How to Design and Introduce Trainer Development Programmes

The Kogan Page Practical Trainer Series

Series Editor: Roger Buckley

PRACTICAL TRAINER SERIES

KOGAN PAGE

How to Design and Introduce Trainer Development Programmes

LESLIE RAE

First published in 1994

Kogan Page Limited
120 Pentonville Road
London N1 9JN

British Library Cataloguing in Publication Data

A CIP record of this book is available from the British Library.

ISBN 0 7494 1400 6

Typeset by Koinonia Ltd, Bury
Printed and bound in Great Britain by
Biddles Ltd, Guildford and King's Lynn

Contents

Series Editor's Foreword

Organizations get things done when people do their jobs effectively. To make this happen they need to be well trained. A number of people are likely to be involved in this training by identifying the needs of the organization and of the individual, by selecting or designing appropriate training to meet these needs, by delivering it and assessing how effective it was. It is not only 'professional' or full-time trainers who are involved in this process; personnel managers, line managers, supervisors and job holders are all likely to have a part to play.

This series has been written for all those who get involved with training in some way or another, whether they are senior personnel managers trying to link the goals of the organization with training needs or job holders who have been given responsibility for training newcomers. Therefore, the series is essentially a practical one which focuses on specific aspects of the training function. This is not to say that the theoretical underpinnings of the practical aspects of training are unimportant. Anyone seriously interested in training is strongly encouraged to look beyond 'what to do' and 'how to do it' and to delve into the areas of why things are done in a particular way. The series has become so popular that it is intended to include additional volumes whenever a need is found for practical guidelines in some area of training.

The authors have been selected because they have considerable practical experience. All have shared, at some time, the same difficulties, frustrations and satisfactions of being involved in training and are now in a position to share with others some helpful and practical guidelines.

All of the books in this series give practical advice on a number of training and development activities which illustrate the range of skills that trainers have to exercise. But, where do these skills come from? It now seems to be recognized that technically competent staff need training to become competent supervisors; by the same token, trainers need to follow a programme of training and development in order to become fully competent. This raises the question of who trains the trainers and in what they should be trained.

Leslie Rae provides an answer to these questions. By drawing on many years of experience, he shows that the 'quick fix' approach is inappropriate for the trainer and the organization. Irrespective of their length of initial training, trainer skills need to be developed over a longer period of time. Only when trainers are properly trained can training make the sort of contribution to an organization that many of us lay claim to.

This book provides the foundation and development to implement a successful trainer training programme. It is of value to training departments and also to senior managers keen to assess the return they will get from an investment in training their trainers.

ROGER BUCKLEY

Preface

The training of trainers has been a major professional interest of mine for some considerable time, principally because of its important role as the essential initial element in the chain of training all other members of a workforce. Some organizations still believe that a newly appointed trainer requires a minimum of formal training – one and a half days is frequently stated as an effective period! My approach, which I believe is in line with the more enlightened trainer-employing organizations, is that a much firmer base should be laid, a programme of development rather than a course, extending over a period of at least one year, with the full range of learning techniques and approaches described in the TDLB NVQ.

This book consolidates this developmental programme theme and can be viewed as a valuable complement and supplement to *The Trainer Development Programme* (Rae, 1994) published by Kogan Page, which describes in detail the material and form which can be used in an effective trainer development programme. I describe it as 'effective' because it follows a pattern which I, my colleagues and my consultancy clients have implemented successfully on numerous occasions. However, the present book also stands alone as a guide to those responsible for designing and implementing trainer development programmes.

I am particularly grateful to the Inland Revenue Training Office with whom I have worked closely as a consultant designing, writing, helping to implement and evaluating a trainer development programme very similar to the programme described here and in my earlier book. This trainer development programme is linked with the entry of the Inland Revenue into the area of TDLB NVQ awards. The Inland Revenue staff with whom I had constant and valuable contact included Tony Ashwick, David Ellis, Annie Moody, Val Townend and Steve Westwood. We used each other's material freely, modifying, varying, rewriting, redesigning until we felt we had the programme somewhere approaching the right stage.

My own views are consolidations of approaches, techniques, methods, attitudes and material developed over more than 20 years and the result of a two-way flow of action and reaction with the many trainers and learner-trainers with whom I have worked, whom I have trained and who have trained me. In the latter case I must mention Dr Peter Honey whose views, attitudes and approaches to training had a considerable impact on my own.

I must thank Dolores Black and her colleagues at Kogan Page for the tremendous support they gave me in the production of this book.

Finally, I dedicate the book to my supportive family – my wife Susan, sons Alex and Oliver, my daughter Aldyth and my one (at present) grand-daughter Sophie.

Leslie Rae

Introduction

Training and development are well-established practices now, and more and more organizations are accepting the fact that a well-trained, skilled workforce at all levels is essential not only for growth, but even survival. The long-established practice of large organizations giving people skills only to lose them to smaller firms who are unable (or unwilling) to provide this training themselves still exists. But even this practice is tending to reduce as individual organizations become more specialized and skills are not necessarily so easily transferable. The increasing recognition of the value of training and development has been observed during the recent UK economic depression and slow recovery when, unlike during previous similar situations, training departments have not suffered the usual savage cuts more than other occupational areas.

If there is to be the required supply of training and development events to satisfy the needs of a well-trained workforce, there must also be a steady supply of skilled trainers. Training in many organizations is seen as a temporary role for staff moving through and up the organization. Few organizations encourage people to stay too long in the role, even fewer having a progress ladder with training and development, and many draw their trainers from the management and supervisory levels for two or three years. This attitude and practice is not all wrong. It is only too easy for trainers to build ivory towers for themselves, to lose touch with an evolving organization, its systems, methods and policy and, if they are interested in personal progress, to become lost in the career 'backwater' (not my word) of the company. The possible temporary nature of the training role, however, can encourage companies with an eye to saving money, to refrain from giving their trainers an effective training 'as they won't be on that job for very long'.

Fortunately many organizations do realize that if their learners are to be developed effectively, their trainers and mentors must possess a substantial and wide range of skills. Some of this can be obtained over a period by means of extended experience, but even this is only partially effective and can occupy a considerable period of time. Experience over time is no guarantee of skill progression, and indeed experience without training can result in the development of bad habits and inefficient ways of working.

In order to avoid these traps, people who enter training for the first time have a much better chance of successful development if they start with an effective training programme, followed by training and line support, practical experience and self-motivated development.

Organizations with training departments sufficiently large can readily support their own trainer development programmes (TDPs) with TDP trainers sufficiently skilled to train and develop their training force. Smaller organizations have at least four options. One can be to have trained, but part-time TDP trainers available at the infrequent intervals that new trainers appear. Another can be to send individual trainers to external organizations that offer trainer training. A third option that is becoming more attractive to smaller firms is to band together to provide a training group which can learn together at a lower cost to individual employers rather than send the learners to an expensive, external provider. A final option, particularly for lone trainers, is to follow one of the open learning packages becoming available. These latter, like direct training courses, have a wide range of methods and acceptability, the more effective ones relying not only on text-based material, but including computer-based training material, interactive video programs, practical projects, tutorials and occasional group events. These packages, like good books on the subject, can provide a good, basic grounding in the theories of learning and training and act as introductions to the many models relating to training and development. But, as with many people skills, there is no complete alternative to practical application under skilled, expert supervision and observation. An effective, direct training programme can provide these with the relevant feedback in the one event without the interruptions of the open learning approach and in a relatively safe, almost real-life environment.

Book Structure

Who is it for?

This book describes the process of developing a TDP by considering the essential content of such a programme and how it can be contained within an effective event or series of events. The primary audience for the book is anyone who is involved in producing development for new trainers or those with some experience but who have had little or no professional training. The training programme producer might be concerned with new trainers within his or her own organization, within a group of companies, or with a small-company network. Training managers and other line managers who have new trainers will be able to identify learning areas for these people and help them to start on the learning development path. The book will also give guidance to them in confirming whether their trainer training providers, internal or external, are offering relevant and quality material. Part-time trainers, lone trainers and staff who have to take part occasionally in the training function can identify the areas in which they have to become competent, consider the range of techniques and methods involved, and also consider what practical steps they have to take to extend the theoretical aspects, whether by obtaining training or by self-development.

This book will also be useful to senior management who are considering the introduction or further employment of staff in the training function, in demonstrating the essential development requirements. Finally, it will show a budding trainer the basic aspects of the training function which they will quickly have to assimilate.

What is the content?

The concept and philosophy of the book are based on:

- the techniques, methods and skills required by a new trainer in the early periods of their role
- a restriction to what is needed immediately and in the relatively short term by a new trainer, rather than 'here's everything you'll ever need'
- the competence standards and requirements of the Training and Development Lead Body's National Vocational Qualification, Level 3
- TDP which will be carried out over two separate weeks with interim practice at work
- a training/learning approach of a mixture of input sessions, discussions, small group activities, exercises, videos, role plays and presentations. The practical use of this range of approaches within the TDP will help to demonstrate the range of approaches to the learners during and as part of their learning process.

Throughout the text are boxed 'design applications' which suggest practical activities related to the accompanying text. These practical activities can be included on a TDP, but they can also be used, sometimes with necessary modification, by lone learners or small self-help groups.

As suggested above, the book's content is based on the philosophy of including initial TDP skills required immediately by the new trainer, to enable them to start functioning in their role, rather than to include virtually every skill used by a trainer, *whether or not the new trainers would need these skills in the early stages of their role function.* This can be considered the basic criterion for the training content of the book and the recommendation for its inclusion in a TDP.

The Training and Development NVQ

The National Vocational Qualification (NVQ) of the Training and Development Lead Body (TDLB) offers excellent guidelines for the areas in which a trainer will have to achieve eventual competence. The content of the recommended TDP is based on this TDNVQ Level 3 with the constraints of the initial requirements of the new trainer. Further competences will be developed with experience and further training as necessary.

The suggested two-week TDP should not be looked on as the beginning and end of a trainer's training. Development must be progressive and further support must be given in both the real world of work as practice and discussion, and in further developmental learning by training events or self-development approaches.

The most important aspect of this support must be with the involvement of the learner's line manager. The learner must be given encouragement and opportunity to practise not only the learned skills, but to experiment, under guidance, with additional and alternative techniques. A planned programme of progressive learning should be agreed and implemented. The TDP should support this programme and should offer a series of short modules on subjects not included in the initial event, but necessary for the rounding of the trainer's skills. These modules should be linked with the NVQ competences in which the trainer is destined to become involved.

The Recommended Format

The recommended TDP format follows the pattern described above, namely two one-week workshops separated by about two months. The appendix suggests a detailed programme for these workshops.

Within the TDP emphasis is placed on the practical presentation sessions – a training approach very frequently used in training events – but with encouragement to approach these presentations in an innovative manner. The learners on a TDP would be encouraged to use the wide range of techniques, methods, approaches and resources to avoid lecture-style presentations. The final presentation on the second workshop acts as a validation of the programme and the learning achieved.

It is obviously not possible in a book of this size to describe in detail all the material which should be included in the programme, but all the topics suitable for inclusion in a TDP are mentioned to a greater or lesser extent with guidance on session content and method of presentation. There is a recommended reading list which will lead you to sources of more detailed information.

Although this is essentially a stand-alone book, it can also be considered as complementary and supplementary to *The Trainer Development Programme* (Rae, 1994) which is a detailed step-by-step manual of material with which to produce a TDP. Many of the activities and instruments mentioned or described briefly in this book are given with full detail in the manual which is formatted on a 23-session, two one-week workshops TDP.

1 Induction

▷   CHAPTER SUMMARY   ◁

This chapter:

- discusses the requirement for an effective induction programme
- demonstrates three induction approaches
- recommends an induction open learning pack and gives guidelines for items to include.

Planning and Design

When the subject of trainer development is raised, the automatic first thoughts are frequently concerned with – what sort of course shall we put on, what should go into the course, and so on – all the necessary elements of planning and design. But as with any training, that for the development of new trainers should start some time before the beginning of the training event.

The training department responsible for trainer development should be on any list held by Personnel so that it might be notified immediately when a new trainer is appointed. At this early stage, arrangements should be made with the new trainers and their line managers for attendance of the trainers at the first available TDP. In some organizations these can occur frequently so that no new trainer need wait very long before a training place becomes available – one aim, depending on circumstances, should be that the interval between appointment and training course should be no longer than two months, but it is impossible to be absolute about this because of the many variables. Although some new trainers, particularly those in smaller organizations where in-house pro-grammes are not frequent, or external courses are not readily available, may have to wait this length of time, or longer, it is preferable that the trainer attends a programme before 'going public'. Untold damage can be caused to both trainer and learners if an inexperienced and not too capable trainer is let loose on a group of learners, particularly if the learners are 'hard' ones. Ideally the logical development path for a new trainer should be:

1. Appointment
2. Immediate arrangement for early training
3. Planned induction or familiarization in the intervening period
4. Training with linked practice in the developing skills
5. Further training
6. Further practice with progressive development in 'real' training
7. Advanced training as this becomes necessary or desirable
8. Development through experience
9. Progression through training requiring increased skills.

Unfortunately this logical process is not always available, but it is a model which learner trainers and their managers should strive to attain as far as possible. The last thing that should happen is that the learner is thrown to the lions with no training, preparation or support at all – it does happen!

The Induction Period

The model described above introduces, in addition to training, the process of induction. Anyone entering a new post, role or career should undergo some form of induction and the new trainer is certainly no exception. In fact, this process is one valuable way of making the period before formal training starts a useful experience which sets a firm seal on the role entry.

At least three effective options are available for the induction process.

Planned at-work development

In this option it is desirable if not essential that the new trainer's line manager should be at least a training manager or personnel manager with responsibility for an experience of training. There may, however, be a senior trainer between the learner and the manager who will be responsible for the process.

- The learner should be made fully aware from the earliest point possible of the stages ahead. The line manager having arranged environmental induction – seating, toilets, canteen etc – should meet promptly with the new trainer, discuss and agree the process and identify another trainer who will be the learner's mentor and guide. At no time should the learners be left to their own devices, unless this is a planned period during which the learner is expected to perform a number of information-gathering activities under their own steam. Even though the learner may be joining a training team, one experienced trainer should be identified as the mentor-guide so that the learners know to whom they should go for information, advice and guidance. In this way a realistic working relationship can be constructed, with advantages for both the learner and the experienced trainer.

- At an early stage the new trainer should be given a detailed, planned programme of progression and involvement in the work of the department. Some time can be usefully allocated for the learner to do some reading – training skills books, training journals, department and organization vision and policy statements – and talking with other trainers; a period of general familarization.

- The next stage for the learners is to sit in, preferably as a student, on some of the training courses, ideally those with which the learner will eventually become involved. Subsequent 'sit ins' should be arranged in a logical programme, first with the learner as a non-participating observer and note-taker – the earlier sit in as student will have acquainted the learner with the material generally; now he or she has to become much more familiar with the material in detail and the processes used in the training event.

- At the next stage the learner will, in tandem with an experienced trainer, start to become practically involved in the training, perhaps by presenting one or two of the more straightforward sessions, under supervision and with support. Progressively the learner should take on more and more training responsibility with the authority to make changes to suit his or her manner and approach. The learner should have the opportunity, if possible, during this period to observe a number of experienced trainers to see the different styles employed by different people.

- During this induction period for the learner trainer, a TDP should ideally be made available at a fairly early stage and there should be no barriers placed in the way of the learner attending to give them an opportunity to learn the widest possible skills and build confidence to take on a more responsible training role.

Induction training

It would be satisfying to know that all new entrants to whatever role or discipline receive an effective induction at the start of their employment and that organizations make time readily available for this purpose. Would that it were so! Many new or transferred workers are expected to induct themselves automatically in the course of the early stages of their work and while immersed in that work.

Some organizations have sufficient new entrants to allow groups to follow an induction training course. There is a wide variety of induction courses and the training literature gives some examples (see, for example, *How to Design and Deliver Induction Programmes*, Michael Meighan, Kogan Page, 1991).

Naturally, if a group of new trainers starts at the same time, the induction training can be customized for this group. But it is more usual for a number of disparate disciplines to be catered for in a general induction programme. In these cases, there is usually a common core of general induction topics related to the organization – contracts, services, grievance and discipline procedures, and so on. But for part of the time, each discipline can be following induction related to its own group; the learners can be following a guided programme of obtaining relevant information.

Inputs to the programme can be made by a section head such as an experienced trainer and the trainees can undertake projects specific to their roles – for example, finding out how trainees are selected in the organization, called to training courses, administered, followed-up and so on, while new entrants to Personnel, for example, are discovering aspects particular to personnel work.

Induction self-learning

Mention was made earlier of the desirability of arrangements being made for the induction of a new trainer rather than their being left entirely to their own devices. However, if self-learning is directed it can be a valuable induction process. Two principal criteria relate to this approach:

- The learner must be given guidance on the path to take for effective induction
- Sufficient time, without interruptions, must be allocated so that the learner can perform what is necessary.

In the more effective cases, the learner is pointed along the road by means of an open learning, self-discovery pack, worked through with the support of his or her new peers and/or line manager. The range of this pack can be quite extensive, but it must be constructed with the particular organization in mind and the time the learner is likely to have made available.

First steps

As in the case of other approaches for new trainer induction, an agreement must have been made with Personnel for the department responsible for offering TDPs to be notified of the details as soon as a new trainer appointment has been confirmed. Arrangements can then be made for the newcomer to be sent an open learning induction pack prior to attending the TDP. At the same time, the line manager can be sent a manager's guide describing what material the learner has received, what is expected of the line manager in terms of support, and seeking confirmation of the TDP arrangements proposed.

The Open Learning Induction Pack

What is included in the induction pack will vary from organization to organization and can be prepared either by the TDP department itself, by an Open Learning department if one exists, or by an organization external to the employing organization.

An induction pack could include:

- A description of the organization's training department, its aims and its place in the organization. The learner can be asked to research this information from leading questions and by talking to other trainers and the training manager.
- A list of questions for the learner to obtain answers:
  - what training does the department offer?
  - why is this training offered?
  - to whom is the training available?
  - how are learners identified and called-up?
  - what other processes are in operation, eg line manager briefings and debriefings?
  - who are the relevant trainers and who does what?
  - what induction process will be followed and who will be responsible?
  - what will be expected of the learner in this process? and so on.
- Other questions which will be linked to environmental aspects are:
  - what training facilities are there?
  - what type of equipment is available?

- how are training materials obtained?
- what type of equipment will the learner be expected to use?
- what forms of brief/scripts are used and how flexible are they?
- what training ethos has to be followed – lectures, discussions, activities, etc?

Lists of this nature can become very extensive and the constructor must take care not to overload the learner, taking into account the time that will be available or is recommended.

- Information should be given about what the learner might expect in terms of recognition and what they should seek themselves. Brief descriptions, amplified in appendices, should be given about professional qualifications available – certainly those such as professional memberships (Institute of Personnel and Development), TDLB NVQs, and other higher qualifications such as MPhil/MEd, etc in training and development. Too much information should not be given as the learners are not at a stage when these qualifications are normally relevant, but they should be made aware of future possibilities and the need to build up evidence portfolios from the start of their period as a trainer.
- New trainers have commented that a useful inclusion in the pack is a sheet prepared for the addition of names, addresses, roles and telephone/fax numbers of useful contacts and in particular the other learner trainers they will be with during the various stages of the direct training programme. This can be particularly useful if the learners are to be located in different places; and the exchange of information can be the start of a supportive network of peers.
- Finally, the subject of learning logs and progressive assessment schemes can be introduced so that the learners might:
  - start constructing and maintaining learning logs from the start of their careers (including the induction period)
  - be aware of what assessments will be expected during, say, the first year of their new function.

The learning log can be completed during the induction to record aspects of relevant learning during that time in preparation for the training courses and eventually more extended learning situations.

An example of a learning log is included in *The Trainer Development Programme* (Rae, Kogan Page, 1994). The log can be used during induction and during subsequent training courses of the TDP. The pages can be extracted from the induction pack (if it is in a ring-binder format) and transferred to another ring-binder which can be a permanent home for these log sheets and future ones. The learners should be encouraged to continue the use of learning logs beyond training as part of their progressive professional development.

Action Requests

As the induction pack is the first part of the TDP, and the learners receiving it will also be invited to the first part of this TDP, the pack can be a useful vehicle in which to suggest what the learner can do prior to attending the programme.

These requirements will vary from organization to organization, but they commonly ask the learner to undertake a project which might involve reading selected training texts, producing hierarchy matrices, identifying their future job description, considering their training needs and so on.

The TDP that I recommend includes in the first week of two week-long workshops, two presentations by each learner. The first presentation, of ten minutes, has to be selected from a list of training subjects and researched prior to the workshop. The suggested list can be sent with the induction pack and a list of recommended training books which will help in the research. The second presentation is over a longer period and is usually a subject chosen by the learner. The learner is advised to think about the subject and the presentation they wish to make and collect any visual aids they might need. This information can also be sent with the induction pack to give the learner time to consider the presentation.

2 Trainer Functions and Roles

$\triangleright$ CHAPTER SUMMARY $\triangleleft$

This chapter:

- identifies and discusses the range of training functions found in training and development, from general job skills training to open learning authoring, CBT/CAT production and coaching and mentoring
- identifies and discusses the various roles that a trainer might be called upon to perform
- identifies possible conflicts between the role of a trainer and the demands of the organization by which he or she is employed and uses the Training Quadrant for this purpose
- concludes with an investigation of the avenues available to a trainer when the personal role preferences and the demands of the organization do not match.

Introduction

The training of trainers must be one of the most important roles in which a trainer can operate. A trainer of people at whatever level has a serious responsibility to both the individuals and the organization; this places a burden on the TDP trainer, but it also means that the role offers a considerable degree of satisfaction in terms of highly applicable training, the development of people and the opportunity to work with people who are in a similar role. This is quite different from the training situations when the 'trainer' is helping, say, supervisors and managers to learn new skills. Although the trainer may have been, and in fact may still be a manager, there is a basic role difference during this latter training which is not evident in trainer training.

Apart from a role empathy, much of the satisfaction stems from the knowledge that new trainers are being helped to adjust to their role, or existing trainers are having their skills developed, both with the end result of an improved ability to help the people that they have to train in their turn. Without training, in some form or other, few new skills or tasks would be implemented or existing skills and tasks developed as necessary. Of course, training whether for skills, knowledge or attitude is not the realm of the trainer alone – managers, supervisors, occasional trainers, experienced staff all have a place in such forms of 'training' as coaching, mentoring, direct job instruction and so on. But most development involves some form of training and learning in their widest definitions. The majority of people have been exposed to some form of training/learning and, hopefully, if a trainer has been involved, the learning experience has been effective with the trainer contributing to this effectiveness.

As a result of this wide need for trainer support in the learning process, the skills of the trainer must be extensive and of a high standard, a competence level attainable only with expert advice, guidance, support and training. Hence the high value of trainer development programmes.

What is Training?

This book concentrates on the training of new trainers by means of trainer training/learning events, usually a training course or workshop. Many of the features discussed can, however, also be applied in either small group training or even self-learning for managers and supervisors who act as occasional trainers or in a limited training position with their own staff. Whatever the training, a description of the process will include its aim to help learners to develop new or advanced skills, areas of knowledge or attitudes using the most relevant approaches and techniques.

Trainer training as a specific, sets out to enable new trainers to learn the basic techniques and approaches of training or to enable existing trainers to develop the training skills they already possess. These new or improved skills are used to carry out one or more forms of training to enable others to develop skills, knowledge and attitudes.

It is necessary in trainer training to ensure that learners are fully aware of the wide-ranging definition of the word and the methods of implementing it. Too often trainers immediately and only think of a training course when a training need has to be satisfied. An effective trainer development programme must ensure that this restricted approach is widened as far as possible.

Training Functions

The width of the range of training functions has been mentioned above and equally, the demands on a trainer can extend from a singular function to one demanding several reasonably disparate approaches. Large organizations often require their trainers to specialize to a lesser or greater extent and here individual trainers may not experience the full range of a trainer's hypothetical role. This restriction may have implications if the trainers are seeking a professional qualification – a subject discussed in Chapter 4.

Smaller organizations frequently employ only one trainer, 'the lone trainer', who may be required to carry out a full or extended range of training, even including administration and authoring work.

The training functions most commonly found are included in the following summary although frequently some are amalgamated for skill requirement or perhaps simple expediency.

General Job Skills Training

Staff at all levels frequently have common problems or needs in order to carry out their jobs effectively. Training programmes to meet these needs can be concerned with such subjects as problem-solving and decision-making, presentational skills, negotiation skills, report writing, and so on. The range is wide and is frequently covered by a number of specific subject modules, although marathon programmes still exist in which many of these subjects are put together as, for example, a 'management course'. The module approach requires a high degree of knowledge and skill on the part of the trainers, and requires above all trainer skills in presenting subjects to managers who do not want all the subjects and may resist the training situation as a result.

Functional Job Skills Training

Organizations frequently introduce new or revised operating systems, procedures and so on, and if these affect numbers of staff, training courses are introduced to help in the implementation. Or similar courses may be produced for existing systems when a number of new employees have this common requirement. Also, similar courses can be held for groups of existing workers who may have common remedial problems in these functional areas. If learner numbers are small, an alternative approach may be 'on-the-job training'.

On-the-job-training

This usually refers to face-to-face, individual training or instruction at the workplace, usually at the workstation itself. Once referred to as 'sitting with Nellie', in its effective form it involves the learner spending some time with an experienced worker who is not only able to perform the job efficiently, but is also able to teach the learner how to do it. This is the alternative to letting the learner sit beside the worker to observe them at work with the hope that they will pick up the skill in time.

Technical Skills Training

This generally refers to training in the IT and computer area where specific technical and technological skills are required. The trainer will usually be a IT/computer expert, but this, like 'Nellie', is not the only requirement. In addition to their personal skill they must also have all the skills of a trainer – the only difference is one of specialization.

Professional Skills Training

Where the organization employs professional staff – accountants, surveyors, auditors, architects, etc – it may provide training and education for these employees to gain professional qualifications and/or to improve on those already held. Depending on the size of the organization and the particular professional skill, this training may take place in-company, but employees are also supported in following these professional requirements in external institutions. Trainer training can be considered in this area where the basic training skill is provided either in-company or externally and development is supported either in-company or externally, or a mixture of the two.

Management Training

Trainers in many larger companies specialize in management training and development. This is usually an extension of general and job-specific skills training, but practised at a higher and more complex level. The more specific management role requirements such as people management, budgetary assessment and control and strategic administration are included in this category.

Trainer Training

The training and development of people who are becoming trainers themselves or require advanced skills in their existing training role – trainer training – can be considered in the professional training function or as a separate function. Trainers involved in trainer development programmes are frequently those who have operated in other training function areas and have progressed sufficiently in their training skills, attitudes and personal roles to enable them to present training courses to other trainers.

Instructional Design

Although not a direct training function, this training application can be described as the 'backroom' aspect of training. Not every trainer has the time or skills to design and produce acceptable training material, such as complete courses, session briefs or scripts, handouts and audio/visual aids. For those who have, this aspect of training can become a specialized service to the front-line trainers.

Open Learning or Resource-based Learning

Known variously by these titles or others, most commonly 'distance learning' or 'open learning', this form of training is through learner self-instruction, usually at the workplace, on an individual basis. Learning packages which may include one or more of text-based instruction, videos, computer programs, interactive video and the like are used in place of trainer/learner face-to-face training.

CBT or CAT

These abbreviations are becoming more common in training and reflect the increasing use of computers and computer programs in training, usually on a self-instructional basis. CBT – computer-based training – is generally used to describe a distance learning package centred around a computer program. CAT/CAL – computer-assisted training/learning' – is a more general training programme, but one in which computers play a major role. Linked with the above are interactive video programmes, the combination of a video with a computer program as a self-instruction programme in which the learner engages in a pseudo dialogue with the video/computer. This is a developing area with more and more sophisticated approaches appearing almost yearly.

Both open learning and CBT/CAT can rarely be stand-alone approaches to learning, requiring the support to a greater or lesser extent of a trainer or other person with some training skills. Although these approaches are highly flexible and adjustable to personal needs, questions or difficulties may arise that the programme cannot resolve – the background 'expert' can then be called upon for assistance or advice.

Coaching

This is a technique which, although not generally a training department function, is one of the most important and successful training techniques. It involves the learner achieving the learning requirements while at work, using real work as the learning vehicle. This progress is the responsibility of the coach who is usually the worker's line manager who agrees a progressive programme of training and development, supports the learning and reviews the process on a continuous basis.

Mentoring

This is a technique similar to coaching. The learner is 'attached' to another person, who is often a more senior colleague but could also be a peer colleague and may frequently be the learner's line manager. The mentor can be responsible for a planned programme of self-learning by the learner, can be shadowed by the learner, or act as controller of a variety of approaches to ensure learning progress.

DESIGN APPLICATION 1

A useful inclusion in a TDP can be, through sub-group or syndicate working, to ask the learners to produce a list similar to the one above rather than be presented with it in input form, to have each learner identify his or her role from the list, and discuss the implications of the range and the restrictions.

Trainer Roles

It has been suggested earlier that definitions of training and development vary considerably; so do the titles of people involved in the process. For example, 'training manager' can mean different things to different people. Sometimes the title is descriptive of the role function, sometimes it is almost at variance with what would be considered common practice or common understanding, and at other times it is a title chosen merely for the sake of having one. The variations are often determined by tradition, misunderstanding or the vagaries of the organization (or individuals within it). Some titles that the new trainer will find in use are given below.

Instructor

The title for this training role is generally taken to imply training in which the approach is directive and usually based on systems and practices which are formalized and fairly inflexible. Practical application is generally in the form of lectures and demonstrations and allows little scope for discussion or the expression of the views or feelings of the learners. However, in some organizations 'instructor' is synonymous with 'trainer' although in such cases the culture of the organization is frequently one of training instruction rather than learner learning.

Trainer, Training Officer, Tutor

These are titles which are interchangeable and are in very general use, often to describe anyone in the field of training. They are frequently interchangeable with 'instructor'. Trainers are found in skills and functional training, management and trainer training and can also have within their job roles the design and production of training events, sessions, training materials and open learning programmes where these are not separate functions. They can also act as the base support tutor for distance learning programmes.

One-to-one Instructor

The one-to-one instructor either takes on the role of 'Nellie' or otherwise acts as instructor to one other person. Such roles are more usually found in small establishments in which the intake of new workers requiring training is small, too small to require larger group instruction. The training itself is usually concerned with systems, procedures or operations, tasks with which the learner is to be directly involved.

Internal Trainer, etc

This refers to the employee(s) in the organization who is responsible for performing the various training and development functions. This will be linked with a specific function or functions.

External Trainer

This is a trainer from another, usually independent, organization which either provides training events to which company employees go, or which brings training into the organization on a contracted basis.

Consultant

A term that is frequently loosely used and which describes an external person or organization which comes to the contracting organization to advise (in this particular case) on training problems and to recommend solutions. The consultant may follow this action by providing the recommended training itself. The loose definition of the term in training and development frequently describes a person or organization that provides training at the request of a client organization without any prior investigation.

Open Learning Author/Writer

Frequently not a direct trainer, this is someone skilled and experienced in writing open learning programmes, instructional texts, computer programs and the like. Large organizations often have separate departments for this purpose which contract with the training department to supply the relevant material. Although the trend is to develop these areas as ones separate from the direct training function, many 'trainers' are still called upon to perform the function in addition to their direct training. In fact, many trainers prefer to do this themselves as they are frequently the ones called upon to support the programmes.

DESIGN APPLICATION 2

As in the case of the discussion on training functions, the practical application of this type of material in a TDP can be most usefully included by encouraging the learners to identify the titles in use, what they understand by the terms, where they stand themselves, and to discuss the implications of what emerges.

Trainer Typology and Links with Organizations and Individuals

We have considered above how the title of a person in training and their allotted function can hide a wide range of practices. What a trainer actually knows, feels and does is much more important than the name. Equally relevant is whether the trainer has motivations and performs actions that may be at variance with the needs and/or requirements of the learner and the organization.

If we consider first the linking of the trainer with the learner, some trainers will be in tune with the needs and attitudes of the learners with whom they are working. Others will know what they want/have to put over and go ahead whether this is in line with the learners' needs or not. There are many variations in this area.

Some trainers will be performing the job because they have been told to do so – today a supervisor/manager, tomorrow a trainer with a group of learners. Others, hopefully the majority, will be in training because they have an empathy with the learners and their needs and want to help them. Yet others are in the role so that they can satisfy a particular ego-need (whether they realize it or not). Some trainers will be training in a manner which suits their style and preferences; others will have to subsume their own preferences to perform training within the organizational regime.

There will be effective trainers, moderate trainers and poor trainers, whether these levels of skill have been reached with or without training. Some trainers are naturals, others reach a competence level only through hard work and experience. Others never reach this level, whether or not they are aware of their limitations.

Organizational Relevance

Some trainer role idenification instruments reflect the trainer types and how these people relate to trainers in a learning situation. But organizations employ trainers to teach their employees what they feel is necessary and normally will require their trainers to conform with the culture, needs and attitudes of the organization. Some trainers can and will adapt, others, perhaps because of effective selection or cultural development, are naturally in tune with the corporate needs. Factors relating to these demands include the:

- organizational culture and tradition
- environmental rigidity or flexibility
- nature of the training
- trainer 'toolkit' available
- trainer's preferred style
- ability to perform in other styles
- trainer's acceptance of use of other styles
- learning preference of the learners.

The Training Quadrant

Hopefully the role requirements of both the trainer and the organization correlate. *The Training Quadrant* (Bennett, Jones and Pettigrew, MSC/ITD Guide to Trainer Effectiveness, 1984) identifies four predominant types of trainer and training situations by comparing individual attitudes to:

- organizational maintenance orientation
- organizational change orientation

with

- traditional educational orientation
- interventionist orientation.

DESIGN APPLICATION 3

The Training Quadrant can be used in a TDP by posing simple questions to the learners about their preferences:

1. Do you have an orientation to the maintenance needs of your organization, ie to ensure the continuance of the existing activities, products or services? Or do you have an orientation to bringing about change within the organization, ie to ensure that training can respond to pressures for change from both outside and inside the organization to help it meet new situations, objectives, etc? Mark on the scale below where you think you are:

Maintenance							Change			
Orientation							Orientation			
0	1	2	3	4	5	6	7	8	9	10

2. Do you have an orientation to traditional methods of training, ie methods and approaches based on the educational or professional model of training, using largely classroom-oriented techniques? Or do you have an orientation to intervention methods, ie bringing a change agent approach to training that involves greater participation by the learners and experiential practices bringing about changes in systems, procedures or technologies and peoples' attitudes and approaches to work? Mark on the scale where you think you are:

Traditional Educational							Interventionist			
Orientation							Orientation			
0	1	2	3	4	5	6	7	8	9	10

3. Answer questions 1 and 2 as far as you see the attitude of the organization for whom you train. How divergent are the two sets of scores?

4. The scores can be transferred to a graphic matrix for easier comparison (see the original source quoted above, or *The Trainer Development Programme*, Rae, Kogan Page, 1994 for this scale).

5. A discussion can be held with the learners comparing the responses and discussing actions that might be necessary.

The answers to the questions given above will identify the responder as falling to a greater or lesser extent in one of four main categories defined by the orientations:

- traditionalist educational orientation and maintenance orientation will identify the *caretaker*.
- traditionalist educational orientation and change orientation will identify the *educator*.
- interventionist orientation and maintenance orientation will identify the *evangelist*.
- interventionist orientation and change orientation will identify the *innovator*.

The *caretaker* is more concerned with a traditional approach to maintaining the existing situation – formal, traditional training following a set training programme which changes only slightly over time.

The *educator* similarly follows a traditional pattern of training techniques and methods, but is more interested in the development of the organization through change. Hence innovative programmes will be introduced, but carefully and traditionally. This style can be rejected as insufficiently varied and innovative and too 'educative' by the learners themselves.

The *evangelist* is a rather strange mixture of innovating methods and techniques, but at the same time trying to maintain a steady, almost traditional environment within the organization.

The *innovator* takes the organizational change aspect of the *educator* further and in an interventionist manner produces flexible, proactive approaches and is the type required by progressive organizations. The danger with this type is that so much change might be proposed that the whole approach is rejected through the natural fear of change.

In any discussion about training style the point must be made that few are 'bad' styles, most of the variety depending for appropriateness on a number of factors. The trainer who is to succeed in any *one* situation must be able to assess that situation and not only decide which style is the most appropriate, but be able to adapt to those requirements.

Trainer Development Programme Design

The aspects of trainer and training functions described in this chapter must be among the initial considerations in the design of a TDP. There is little value in designing a programme for trainers which highlights facilitation, variety of content and approach, creative application and so on when the learners come from an organization that demands their strict adherence to consistency, routine and an organizationally determined mode of approach.

However, the opportunity should not be lost to include in a programme designed for such an organization, the various more adventurous training approaches and techniques. The trainers, slowly if they are new, more positively if they are on a more advanced development programme, may be able to change the organization's attitude.

Certainly, consideration and discussion of questionnaires and actuates leading to an increase in self-awareness and personal/organizational practice should be part of the TDP. This will ensure that the learners are aware of their personal needs as a trainer, how they can approach their role within whatever role boundaries that exist, and to what extent they can introduce the new concepts presented to them. Learners need to ask:

- Who am I?
- What are my trainer beliefs?
- What are the training beliefs of my organization?
- Which approach(es) do I prefer?
- Which approaches do I *have* to accept?
- Can I accept any conflict of interests and preferences?
- *Must* I accept these? If not, what can I do?

3 Trainer Qualities

▷   CHAPTER SUMMARY   ◁

This chapter:

- introduces the concept of qualities necessary for trainer effectiveness
- lists the desirable trainer qualities
- describes the desirable trainer qualities.

What Qualities should a Trainer Have?

Skills can be learned and developed, but the change or development of aptitudes and attitudes is considerably more difficult (some might say impossible). This is reflected in the 'Nellie' syndrome in which it often becomes obvious that the skilled expert in a function cannot teach or train in that area.

Because of this need for an aptitude if the function is to be performed effectively, a trainer must possess not only the skills of the 'trade' (these can be learned), and a personality which is compatible with the approach (perhaps behaviour may be a better word as new behaviours can be developed), but also a difficult to define 'attitude'. Some people are natural trainers requiring only knowledge and skills in the various techniques; others with the techniques will become trainers in a limited sense; others, however much training is given, will never become trainers and, probably realizing this, leave the profession (or should do!).

Some of the personal qualities and general skills of the trainer are included in the following:

Approachable	Articulate
Aware of role requirements	Commitment
Creativity	Credible
Empathic	Enjoys working with people
Enthusiastic	Flexible
Mental agility	Organizational and task/skill knowledge
People skills	Positive attitude
Practises what is preached	Programme skills
Punctual	Resilience
Self-awareness	Self-confident
Self-development motivation	Sense of humour
Sensitivity	Stress management
Training skills and knowledge	Understandable

This list is based on my contact with trainers in TDP events when they were asked to identify the qualities. Obviously not every group identified all the qualities and the list is in no order of priority, priorities varying from group to group.

DESIGN APPLICATION 4

During a TDP workshop, rather than discuss the qualities listed as an input session, it is more interesting for the learners if the list is constructed by asking the learners to produce it, either in the full group or by the sub-group method. The descriptions that follow can be used by the trainer to ensure that all qualities are examined.

Approachable

Unless the training is taking place in a very formal and structured environment, and this is unlikely for a TDP, the trainer must show that he or she can be approached at any time by the learners, both during the training period and out of class. In the latter situation, however, it can be difficult to decide the extent of 'socialization' in which the trainer should become involved. Remember that at times a directive approach may have to be taken.

Articulate

There is little value in having a trainer whose mode of expression or accent are so difficult or extreme that the learners are unable to understand them. Material to be presented to the learners must be sufficiently known by the trainer to enable this material to be expressed in a clear, logical and understandable way.

Aware of Role Requirements

This relates to a clear understanding of the type of trainer role necessary in the particular situation – instructor, facilitator, trainer, etc – and the requirements of the employing organization, either that of the trainer or the learners.

Commitment

It should not be necessary to say that an effective trainer must be committed to the practice of training and the desire to help learners learn. There is always argument about whether the trainer should be fully committed to the subject in which training is being undertaken. There should be no question of this in TDP training, but otherwise if commitment is not complete, the trainer *must* ensure that any personal doubts are not broadcast to the learners in any way.

Creativity

This quality is essential in TDP training in view of the wide mix of techniques, methods and approaches that should be used. Each group will be found to be different in skill, experience and attitude and the trainer must be sufficiently creative to produce activities that are relevant for the particular group.

Credible

The trainer's credibility must not only exist but be evident, otherwise the learners will take insufficient notice of the trainer. Experience of the subject being taught is essential in almost every form of training – a good knowledge of theory does not always sell the message.

Empathic

A trainer, working with a group of learners, needs to have a good awareness of what is going through their minds. This does not involve mind-reading, but an awareness of learners' needs can produce empathy. One of the major aspects of this quality is that the trainer must listen to the learners all the time.

Enjoys Working with People

This is often seen as a trite remark and a trainer/teacher does not need the quality to be effective as long as dislike of people does not become evident. However, if this quality is not present, enjoyment of the job – an essential item in training – will not be present, with unfortunate personal results.

Enthusiastic

Enthusiasm is infectious. A trainer without enthusiasm for what is being presented will be an unhappy trainer and the lack of enthusiasm will soon become evident to the learners – 'If (the trainer) doesn't believe in this, why should we!'.

Flexible

This quality in a trainer links closely with creativity. Every group is different and group commitment can soon disappear if the trainer follows a set programme even when it becomes obvious that variations and modifications are needed.

Mental Agility

This is not only linked with creativity and flexibility but is required, for example, when a trainer is posed a question outside the brief being followed. Decisions must be made immediately whether to respond at once, or delay the answer; to step in or let the process continue during an activity that is going wrong, and so on.

Organizational and Task/Skill Knowledge

Internal trainers will usually be *au fait* with the organization to which they belong, but if the learner group comprises individuals from a number of organizations or the trainer is an external one, a first task for the trainer, prior to the training, must be to gain this knowledge. Similarly, the extent of the tasks and skills in question must be researched. There is no value in training learners in, for example, the use of complex computers and programs if they are not going to have these facilities available at all.

People Skills

Trainers will find that the learning they are seeking to have accepted will occur more readily if they are able to relate effectively to the people who are the learners. This demands people skills, those very difficult skills to define that are concerned with the trainer's behaviour (verbal and non-verbal) with their learners, the abilities to deal with dysfunctional people and considerable persuasive negotiation and influencing skills.

Positive Attitude

This quality links with commitment to the subject being taught in that excessive hesitancy and expressed doubt is unlikely to convert or change learners. If you believe that the technique being considered is the 'best thing since sliced bread' ensure that your attitude expresses this view.

Practises what is Preached

A trainer must be seen to be doing what he or she is putting over to the learners – learning does not succeed with an attitude of 'Don't do as I do, do as I say'. However, no trainer is perfect and must be ready to admit errors or faults to the group and describe their significance.

Programme Skills

Many trainers need to develop training programmes from the start. This demands a skill in designing programmes, understanding which techniques, etc will be effective, how long each item will need/take, whether there are relevant activities and so on.

Punctual

If you want the learners to arrive or return punctually for sessions or activities, you must show an example. If not, late arrival by you will be noticed and reflected in the behaviour of the learners – 'He can't be bothered to get here on time even though we do'.

Resilience

All will not always go well during a training event. The trainer must have sufficient resilience not to let this affect his or her performance and to try to resolve the problem.

Self-awareness

Too often we can think that our behaviour is always appropriate and the reaction of learners is what we want. Is it? Are we sufficiently aware to realize the true state of affairs?

Self-confident

Self-confidence goes hand in hand with many of the other qualities, but is often the result of being aware that you have the relevant techniques and skills, know the material you are to present or make available and have an acceptable behaviour pattern.

Self-development Motivation

Learning is the result of self-induced motivation to learn and as a result, change. The trainer must have this motivation otherwise advances and beneficial changes will be missed – standing still really means moving backwards!

Sense of Humour

This does not mean the ability to tell a string of jokes, but to use situations to ease stress and also to introduce items in a relevant manner. A trainer must also have the ability to laugh at themselves, either overtly with the group, or in private at the end of the day. Inability to do this can cause a lot of unhappiness.

Sensitivity

Sensitivity to what is occurring and the attitudes of the learners at any time is another aspect of awareness which must be developed by the trainer who is to be fully effective and satisfy the needs of the learners as far as possible.

Stress Management

There is no doubt that training is a stressful experience, but this stress must be constrained so that it does not become distress. Learn stress-reducing practices and activities, but never let the importance of the occasion disappear from mind.

Training Skills and Knowledge

This hardly needs comment since if the trainer is not in possession of these to the fullest extent possible, they should not be in training, particularly as a TDP trainer.

Understandable

Jargon, over-strong regional accents, speech disorders, vocal manner-isms, voice volume and so on, tend to reduce the learners' understanding of the trainer. Be aware of your shortcomings – and do something about them.

DESIGN APPLICATION 5

The learners will need to identify their own priorities of the qualities described and at this stage in a programme it can be valuable to introduce an activity to serve this purpose. An activity of this nature can be one which involves the learners identifying priorities from the list in terms of *Most important, Important, Not so important* and *Least important.* Learners, either individually or in small groups, rank the qualities under these headings and discuss the results.

---

4 Trainer Qualifications

⊳   CHAPTER SUMMARY   ⊲

This chapter:

- introduces the concept of assessing trainer tasks with the use of the Training Task Inventory
- describes NVQ qualifications and in particular the Training and Development Lead Body NVQ
- identifies the sources of other training and development professional memberships and qualifications.

Introduction

Trainers, whether new or partly or fully experienced, whatever their personal qualities and attitudes, need to know these aspects of themselves as completely as possible. But an additional requirement is not only what they are and what tasks they can perform, but what tasks their functions contain and how well they have to be able to perform these tasks.

Until fairly recently the task requirement was covered by a 'job description' or 'job specification'. Unfortunately, as with many occupations, these descriptions are not always available, not documented, and are in such a poor format that they are unhelpful in defining the role. Management training has attempted in many cases to improve not only the quality but also the quantity and implementation of realistic descriptions with a practical application – not always successful. It was intended that improved job descriptions would also be valuable in appraisal systems.

There has been considerable improvement in this area in recent years, even in training departments, but my qualitative assessment is that there are still many employees, including trainers, who do not have a realistic, up-to-date job description.

Trainer Tasks

A step forward in the field of training and development was attempted in a co-operation between the Manpower Services Commission (now Employment Department) and the Institute of Training and Development (ITD), the professional institute for trainers, training managers and allied occupations. This co-operation produced the Trainer Task Inventory (TTI) based on original work in the Air Transport and Travel Industry Training Board by Terry Morgan and Martin Costello. When this Board was wound up the then Manpower Services Commission funded Morgan and Costello to complete the work. In June 1984 the MSC and the ITD co-published the inventory (*Guide to Trainer Effectiveness*, Manpower Services Commission and ITD, Crown Copyright, 1984.).

The TTI is essentially a structured task analysis with as full a list as possible of all the tasks carried out by 'trainers'. The tasks are organized into family groups of related tasks, but not necessarily with a particular job holder's role. It can be used with a variety of trainer roles by adding or omitting tasks to produce relevancy.

The Structure of the TTI

The TTI recognises three major levels of activity in a trainer's role, plus a fourth one concerned with a variety of general principles:

- helping people to learn and develop
- helping people to solve performance problems
- helping people to anticipate needs and problems and to formulate policies.

Helping people to learn and develop. The identification of learning and training needs; designing and preparing for training events of whatever nature; instructing or training either face-to-face with individuals or groups, or at a distance by other methods; evaluating the training provided.

Helping people to solve performance problems. Taking the necessary action to identify performance problems amongst the target population; selecting and designing appropriate intervention strategies, implementing the intervention and evaluating the results of the intervention.

Helping people to anticipate needs and problems and to formulate policies. The identification of future needs and problems and the formulation of strategies and plans to deal with these.

General functions. All factors which would support some or all of the other activities – administration, management, knowing the organization and self-development.

The TTI Format

The TTI contains:

- the four levels of activity described above
- a number of work areas within each level of activity
- a number of task groups (or tasks, of which there are 252) within each work area.

An example of a work area is work area 4 which is concerned with *Preparing for training/learning events* and contains the following 23 task groups.

1. Write/update manuals
2. Write programmed texts
3. Write handouts
4. Design visual aids
5. Make visual aids
6. Design audio-visual aids
7. Make audio-visual aids
8. Set up and position audio-visual equipment
9. Repair damaged equipment
10. Purchase training material
11. Negotiate resources/training facilities in hotels
12. Choose outside speakers
13. Brief outside speakers
14. Carry out pre-course interviews with trainees
15. Send out joining instructions
16. Analyse pre-course reports on trainees
17. Test out alternative methods/media
18. Write case studies
19. Investigate ready-made courses/materials
20. Design trainee self-assessment instruments
21. Develop computer-managed instructional material
22. Prepare tape/slide script material
23. Prepare tape/slide visual material

It will be immediately apparent that a number of these tasks are not relevant to some trainers and that there are a number of omissions from a particular trainer's job specification. However, with a core list in evidence it becomes a relatively simple task to add or omit items until it realistically represents the situation.

Using the TTI

Although a number of variations are possible within the use of the TTI, the more normal use is a relatively simple checklist of skills attained from tasks performed.

Identification of task performed

This is a simple approach which shows which tasks are done – not the extent, the level of skill etc – and only has use as a brief form of checklist reminder. In this format it does not identify the level of skill of each item nor when they were performed, but its appeal can be in this very simplicity rather than more complex forms which soon become too much of a chore to complete and maintain.

The TTI is a very flexible instrument; exactly how it is used will depend on the needs of the trainers using it or their line managers.

Work area 4: Preparing for training/learning events

Listed below is a task group and the tasks it includes. Tick against all tasks that you perform. Add at the bottom any tasks you do that are not listed.	
Task group	
1. Write/update manuals etc	

Figure 4.1 *A typical work area*

Competences and National Vocational Qualifications

The TTI, although it is a valuable and useful instrument, is in many ways a crude device. Several years ago the British government made a statement of intention that there would be national standards developed for all occupations. The purpose of these standards was to give assessors in a variety of areas real tools with which to measure the competences of working people at all levels. With the support of the then Training Agency, bodies such as the Management Charter Initiative and the National Council for Vocational Qualifications led the way for standards to be produced.

Competence standards were intended to apply not only to occupations but also industries and sectors. Training and development is one of the areas which crosses industry and sector boundaries and the body developed to establish a framework for training and development competence standards was the Training and Development Lead Body (TDLB). The aim of this body was to produce standards across the profession from training administration, through direct trainers to training managers and human resource managers.

Following the development of competence standards is the creation of a National Vocational Qualification, in this case that for training and development – the Training and Development National Vocational Qualification (TDNVQ). Awarding bodies are authorized to issue these qualifications which are considered at different levels and these now include NCVQ, ScotVec, City and Guilds, ITD and so on. The NVQ for trainers starts at the direct trainer level and is designated Level 3. This level offers statements of competence for training officers or trainers who deliver training specified and designed by others, assess the outcomes of that training and design training from given directives. Level 4 is basically that of the training manager who may also be involved in training and who identifies, designs, delivers and evaluates at the corporate and management level. Level 5 is that of the human resource development manager at the strategic design and delivery of training systems level.

One of the complaints aimed at the TDLB was concerned with the too wide-ranging competence area of Level 3, as far as trainers were concerned. This level includes corporate training needs identification and the design of corporate and organizational strategies. Many trainers are direct trainers, responsible for the tactical design and delivery of training events with little opportunity, if any, for involvement in the wider aspect of training and development. During Spring of 1994 the TDLB conducted research into revising the competences and NVQs and the result of this study is a set of standards couched in less ambiguous and more understandable language, containing units and elements that are more realistic when applied to the functions, and with a revised structure for the unit requirements at the different levels, These new standards came into effect in the latter part of 1994.

NVQs

The basis of an NVQ is known as functional analysis, which takes a holistic approach to the job rather than concentrating on the tasks. The first definition in the analysis is that competence is defined as 'the ability to perform activities within an occupation to the standards expected'. This emphasizes several aspects of competences and NVQs. Obviously the activities performed are to a standard – this is where the NVQ defines these standards and all aspects relating to them. But above all, the NVQ is about performing work, at work, and not a training or education qualification. Naturally training becomes involved – if someone does not have a particular competence that requires a particular skill, they can gain that skill by means of training, followed by *actually performing the tasks at work* to demonstrate that they are capable of achieving the competence standard required.

An NVQ follows this requirement with progressively detailed aspects of the standards.

The key purpose
Any competence standards description, to whatever it refers, must start with a statement of the key purpose of the role. The key purpose for training and development is:

> *Develop human potential to assist organizations and individuals to achieve their objectives.*

Areas of competence
The next level below the key purpose comprises five areas of competence. These are:

Area A: Identify training and development needs
Area B: Plan and design training and development
Area C: Deliver training and development
Area D: Review progress and assess achievement
Area E: Continuously improve the effectiveness of training and development.

Key roles

Each area of competence has from one to four key roles. For example, Area B has three key roles:

Key role B1: Design training and development strategies for organizations

Key role B2: Design training and development programmes

Key role B3: Design and produce learning materials.

Units of competence

The key roles are then divided into units of competence which are the building blocks of an NVQ and for which separate accreditation can be awarded, below the full NVQ. If a trainer cannot be involved in all the unit requirements of an NVQ, assessment of individual units can be made and these can be awarded; eventually when it is possible for the trainer to demonstrate competence in the other units, those already awarded can count towards the NVQ.

Each key role contains a number of units identified by sub-classifications of the key role. For example, key role B3 (Design and produce learning materials) noted above, contains three units:

Unit B31: Design, test and modify training and development

Unit B32: Design, test and modify information technology (IT)-based material

Unit B33: Prepare and develop resources to support learning.

Elements of competence

Each unit is further divided into elements of competence which are the more practical and direct activities within a role. Again, each unit contains a number of elements, identified by a further sub-number of the key role and unit. The units vary in having from two to five elements apiece.

As an example, the elements contained in unit B31 quoted above are:

Element B311: Agree requirements for training and development

Element B312: Design training and development materials

Element B313: Test the design of training and development materials

Element B314: Modify and produce training and development materials.

You will see that the range of elements shown above describes the progressive involvement in that particular competence, from agreeing requirements to producing the end result.

Performance criteria

The units and elements define the standards of competence, but in order to assess an individual's competence against these standards, there must be some mechanism to identify whether the requirements are satisfied. One important part of NVQs is that there are no satisfaction levels of competence – the standard of competence is stated and a person can perform the task to the required standard or they can't.

The performance criteria are in fact statements of the evidence that is required for an assessor to agree the satisfaction of the element. Each element has a number of associated performance criteria, ranging from five to ten or more criteria. If we look at, for example, element B312, the eleven performance criteria for this element are:

Unit B31: Design, test and modify training and development
Element B312: Design training and development materials
Performance criteria:
a) The agreements made with clients for materials are clarified and explained to all those involved in the design process
b) The specific aims and objectives of the materials are clearly identified
c) Possible types of materials, media and delivery methods suitable to the subject matter, learning context and duration are selected
d) Possible design problems are identified and realistic ideas for overcoming them are generated
e) A range of design options is developed and a preferred option selected which meets all specified requirements
f) Materials from external sources are adapted and used within the constraints of copyright law
g) Guidance and instructions on the correct use of the materials are precise and clear
h) Designs are discussed with all relevant people at critical development stages
i) Final design option chosen conforms to the agreements made and meets all specified learning requirements
j) The language, style and format of the materials is appropriate to the learning needs of users
k) Materials are designed within the agreed timescale and resources.

In addition to the performance criteria listed, notes are included in the element giving guidance on the type of evidence – performance and knowledge – required to satisfy the criteria. For the performance criteria described above the evidence required is:

Performance evidence
Records and notes of discussions and agreements on requirements
Designs at different stages of development
Notes of discussions concerning the development of the design.

Knowledge evidence
Principles of design
Methods of differentiating materials to promote achievement of
    objectives
Ways to introduce, promote and negotiate materials with clients
How to design materials to support training and development
How to assess which learning materials are most suited to clients
Common design problems
Examples of good design
Current relevant debates concerning the design and use of training
    and development materials
Copyright requirements
Equal opportunities legislation and good practice
Principles of non-sexist and non-racist language.

Range statements
In order to complete the standards and the guidance on what is required
to assess them, a final section is included in each element – the range
statement. Not every trainer performs the functions described in the
standards. The range statement guides the assessor in a consideration of
the range of contexts and applications in which a competent person
would be expected to achieve the element. In the B312 example, the
range statements include:

2) Purpose of materials: to support learning, for assessment and
    review
4) Materials: packs, individual sheets
6) Guidance and instructions cover: completion instructions, infor-
    mation on learning processes
    and so on.

These items from the key purpose to the range statements describe *all* the
competences that are found in the training and development function.
Obviously one role holder cannot be required to demonstrate or perform all the items – some 5 areas, 13 key roles, 29 units and more than
one hundred elements. The standards form the basis on which NVQs are
built.

Seeking an NVQ award

Trainers who have the required experience and the evidence to support it apply for registration and eventually their portfolio of evidence of competence is assessed by both internal and external assessors and verifiers. If all the requirements are satisfied, a TDNVQ can be awarded by the body through which application has been made, or, as mentioned earlier, individual units can be accredited. Assessment is not necessarily on current or future work: if the requirements have already been met at work in the relatively recent past and there is evidence to support this, prior learning and experience can be accredited towards the award. This suggests that new trainers should be advised to commence a portfolio against the time when they might wish to seek an NVQ award.

The TDLB has developed three levels of NVQ – levels 3, 4 and 5 – and the awarding bodies offer NVQs at these levels based on the units of competence. Each level requires that certain units and parts of units should be demonstrated by the candidate before an NVQ can be awarded. Units are awarded on a unit-by-unit basis until the required selection has been assessed for competence.

The NVQs determined by the 1994 review of standards consist of level 3, Training and Development; level 4, Learning Support; level 4, Human Resource Development; and level 5, Training and Development. Each of these NVQs requires candidates to satisfy unit award in determined selections:

> level 3: Training and Development – 7 core plus 3 optional units
> level 4: Learning Development – 7 core and 5 optional units
> level 4: Human Resource Development – 7 core plus 5 optional units
> level 5: Training and Development – 7 core plus 5 optional units.

The competence of the candidates for an NVQ such as that described above will be assessed by a qualified assessor who will follow the competence-standards requirements described earlier. If a candidate does not have the knowledge or skill required to satisfy part of the requirements, training can help to develop these and the candidates will then be able to practise the skills until they are able to demonstrate the competence. This is the area where training and education can complement the practicality of the NVQ competences, the ability to perform the function to the required level of competence remaining the unique criterion for the award of the NVQ.

Additional or separate unit requirements are provided for standards for competence in assessment and verification and include units D31 to D36, the combination depending on the award sought.

Other Professional Paths

The NVQ approach is not the only qualification/recognition path available to the trainer and new trainers should at least be aware of what is available, so that they might bear this in mind as they develop during their career. Most paths require some prior experience, but the new trainer is advised, as with the NVQ approach, to start planning needs and routes at an early stage and collecting evidence which might be useful in seeking an award etc.

The professional institute for trainers and developers and allied occupations is the Institute of Personnel and Development. In addition to awarding various degrees of membership, the IPD offers certificate courses, awards TDLB NVQs, offers a vacancy service, has a library and bookshop facility and supports a number of training events from time to time.

Membership – currently as either Fellow, Member, Associate Member or Corporate Member – requirements vary from time to time and if the subject was to be raised at a TDP event, the IPD would make available all the current information necessary. Suffice to say that membership brings many advantages to the trainer, new or experienced and it is to be supported.

Other Professional Qualifications

Qualifications other than NVQs are available for people involved in the training world. Although it may be some time before a new trainer is interested in such a qualification or is in a position to apply, they should be given basic information at the early TDP stage so that this can be kept in mind for the future. Portfolio development and continued professional development should be encouraged for the same reason.

The types of other professional qualifications include the following, details of which could be made available during a TDP event.

- Open University degree courses
- University open learning degree courses (for example, the MEd (training and development) course offered by Sheffield University)
- University full-time or part-time courses leading to a degree
- Degree courses offered by other organizations (for example, the MPhil and PhD degrees of membership offered through action learning by the International Management Centres).

- Direct Trainers' Award – Institute of Personnel and Development
- Certificate in Human Resource Development – Institute of Personnel and Development
- Diploma in Human Resource Development – Institute of Personnel and Development
- Master's degree in Human Resource Development – Institute of Personnel and Development

New courses, in addition to new aspects of the NVQ system and its awarding bodies, are appearing all the time; addresses and contacts can be made available to the learners at the time of the TDP event.

5   Adult Learning

$\triangleright$ CHAPTER SUMMARY $\triangleleft$

This chapter:

- describes the barriers to adult learning
- discusses the reasons why and how adults learn
- describes the learning style and preference models of Kolb and of Honey and Mumford and suggests how these can be included effectively in a trainer development programme.

Introduction

Whatever the trainer's skills and knowledge in terms of training approaches, methods and techniques, it is necessary to have the all-embracing skill of communicating with learners. This implies a wide knowledge of the way people learn, the techniques that help this learning and the barriers to learning. Knowledge of these areas and skills in overcoming problems should be an early priority in a trainer development programme, with the principal technique using the learners' own styles, methods and barriers to demonstrate the various aspects. It should then be easier for the learners to relate the problems in particular to their learners in turn.

DESIGN APPLICATION 6

In order to assist in the process of encouraging the learners to relate their own experience of learning to appropriate methods, it can be useful to put the learners into small groups to discuss their recollections of learning (a) at school, (b) at college or university and/or (c) as an adult at work. They can be asked to identify the good and bad points in these learning encounters and express how they would have wished to have been treated.

After the small group discussions, the results can be summarized on a flipchart in a full group session in order to stress the different approaches possible and the flexibility required of the trainer.

The Barriers To Learning

The 'purist' might regard consideration of the barriers inappropriate as a first approach, but the majority of people raise the question of problems first rather than that of appropriate methods.

DESIGN APPLICATION 7

Two principal approaches to identify the barriers to learning are available.

- One uses the combined experience of the learners by placing them in small groups to identify, as many barriers as they can. These would then be listed in plenary session and discussed, with omissions being introduced by the trainer.
- The other is for the trainer to provide this information in the form of a visual aid, to be discussed and added to from the experiences of the learner.

A visual aid concerned with the barriers to learning should include the following, which would be developed in discussion with the learners:

Previous Experience

Most people, whether in education establishments, at work or during adult training events, have experienced episodes which act as a learning barrier. You may have been embarrassed in front of others by the trainer on a course (whether intentionally or otherwise). Such factors can contribute towards an attitude of 'I don't want to learn' and must be broken down by the trainer as soon as there is realization that a problem exists. Of course it is sometimes very difficult to bring the reasons for the barrier to light; they may be more likely to emerge *after* training, in a more social situation.

Lack of Confidence

If learners attending a training event or taking on an open learning package have experienced severe barriers to learning previously, it is possible that they will approach the current event with the feeling that it is going to be too difficult for them. The trainer must ensure that at the start of the learning event the process and content are described fully and the level explained. Doubts should then be sought and clarified; above all, the trainer should ensure that every help will be given to the learners if difficulties are experienced.

A start-of-course knowledge test can often help in this respect, particularly if two tests are given – the first containing questions that the learners should be able to answer (the confidence builder) and the second related more to new material that forms the content of the event. There is, of course, the danger that the second test will reduce the confidence resulting from the first test, but this risk should be minimized by an appropriate introduction.

Lack of Motivation

Motivation is an internally generated attitude and every learner comes to a training event with a range of motivational attitudes and levels. Again, they may have been forced to attend against their wishes. Others may not see the reason for the training. Yet others may feel that they already know what they think the training is going to teach them.

One fact is certain – you cannot motivate people to learn. What you *can* do is provide all the factors available to encourage them to motivate themselves. A logical and acceptable explanation should be given about how the learner will benefit from the new skill, how they will grow as a result of the experience, how their chances of progressing will be enhanced with the learning, and so on.

Fear of Change

Change is frequently an unwanted event, usually because it is feared. Comfort results from acquaintance, fear from a strange situation. The principal purpose of training is to produce change, whether this is the introduction of new material or a development of existing knowledge and skill. Previous changes may have resulted in unwanted results. The training event is frequently too late to modify any such feelings but the trainer can help by describing, at an early stage, what the training involves and why it is taking place.

Fear of Failure

If the fear of change is not a barrier to motivation, the fear of failure (to absorb the training) may be. Fear of failure may be the result of previous failures. The trainer obviously cannot ensure success, but *if* the training has been designed effectively, *if* it is presented effectively, *if* the learners have the motivation and ability to learn, and *if* they have been selected correctly by their line managers, there should be a minimized chance of failure. Whatever the situation, the trainer should ensure that the learners are aware that every help will be given to them to learn. It is not always possible to discount the risk of sanctions – this will depend on the organization and its procedures and attitudes to training.

Old Dog Syndrome

The belief that 'you can't teach old dogs new tricks' is in fact not completely true. If an older person has kept their mind active and in a learning mode, their experience may well mean they are often in a better position to learn than the younger person who has only youth to rely on. Obviously, if an older person has allowed their mind to atrophy, learning is almost impossible. Quite often this syndrome emerges when older workers attend training events during the last few years of their careers: the 'old dog' excuse is used for a variety of other barriers, including 'Why bother at this stage in my life?'.

Lack of Interest

The learner (once again) may have been sent to the course against their will or there may be no sound reason for the new learning. The learner may simply not want to progress and therefore cannot see any personal value in attending.

The wrong learner on the wrong course is not something a trainer can take much responsibility for: any blame is firmly on the head of the line manager, who should also have been aware of the lack of interest (training is expensive enough without taking places for people who will not benefit).

Wrong Techniques of Approach

Even when a training event contains the appropriate material, learners are motivated and the trainer is a skilled presenter, the event can still fail: the method or technique of training may be inappropriate.

If the training event contains the appropriate material, learners are motivated and the right methods are used, learning can still fail through trainer ineptitude unless learner motivation is very high.

Unlearning

Resistance to learning can exist if the potential learners already have experience of the type of material but of an outdated nature. The training will be intended to introduce new systems, procedures or methods, but the earlier knowledge, skills and attitudes have to be cleared before the learners' minds are receptive to the new. Some may resist this unlearning for some of the reasons already discussed, others may find it difficult to clear their minds sufficiently. But if the training is to be effective, the trainer must be sufficiently skilled to ensure that the message is offered and accepted.

How and Why Adults Learn

Dealing with the barriers discussed above also gives a trainer insight into why it is that people do want to learn. Some of the reasons behind the motivation and ability to learn include:

Needing to

Probably the strongest motivational factor for learning is when the learner has a specific need to learn a new skill to preserve job security or to learn the new skills of a different role.

Wanting to

Wanting is frequently linked with needing, but there are occasions when people want to learn, whether for a particular purpose – as described in the 'need' above – or simply for the pleasure of learning something new. Of course somebody may often have to make this desire emerge.

Gaining Some Control

Younger learners are dominated in the majority of cases by the need to learn and are more willing to accept direction and trainer-controlled situations. As people mature, become more experienced and more selective in their learning, they become less willing to be trainer-led all the time and demand that they are given some control over the learning and its event. This factor of course reflects high motivation and is something a trainer should capitalize on – self-learning is a more powerful medium than the necessity of having to learn from someone else. The successful trainer will balance an event so that the control, and hence the maximum learning, is balanced between the trainer and the learners. In learning events of this nature, the trainer question 'How would you like to tackle this?' becomes common.

Experience can be Used and is Valued

When subjects are introduced it is always valuable to seek from the learners the extent of their existing knowledge. Those with knowledge and experience can be used to confirm the techniques proposed and to add complete realism to the training with accounts of their experiences. Using them in this way not only helps the trainer and the learners, but shows the experienced learner that this experience is valued.

Enhanced 'Realism'

The greater the experience, skill and knowledge of the adult learner, the less likely they are to accept training approaches that are not related in some way to their world of work. Even apparently non-work-related activities must be shown to have such a relationship they will be treated as 'games' in the worst sense of the word. Although the activity may not have any obvious work link, this can emerge in the review and feedback session following the activity.

Learning without fear of ridicule or censure

Much more so than with young learners, adult learners have a hatred of being ridiculed or censured in public, in front of their peers, subordinates or senior managers. The atmosphere of the learning event must be developed in such a way that the participants will not hesitate to respond to a question, make a statement or do something in an activity. This can be developed only by showing in the early stages that there are no sanctions. It is often useful for the trainers to put themselves in such a potential position. Encourage laughter *with* people rather than *at* them.

Learning Styles

At one time, training was of a singular nature; the 'trainees' attended a training course and were told in a lecture-type presentation what they had to learn. After the 1939–45 war there was a strong swing to experiential training in which there were few input sessions, but many practical activities. It was eventually realized that neither approach on its own was completely successful and a balanced mixture began to evolve. Such approaches as input sessions, discussions, practical activities, role plays, games, simulations, videos, computer programs and so on all have a place in effective training/learning. This is not to say that they should all be used at once, but the value of each with regard to a particular learning activity should be assessed and the appropriate method(s) implemented.

We can all learn in different ways, even when forced to do so in ways which we do not like. Older readers will recall having to sit and learn arithmetic tables or lists of irregular verbs by repetition. I hated this, but I can still rush through my tables and recite the list of French intransitive verbs of motion! However, because we can learn in these ways, this does not mean that they are the best or most appropriate ones. Research has shown that different people have different preferences for learning methods and learn more easily by some methods than others. There are, of course, restrictions in the number of ways that material can be offered for learning, and in many cases we have to compromise. If for example, someone can learn only by seeing the object itself and this object happens to be located on the other side of the world, it may not be appropriate to take that person 12,000 miles to see the object. We have to be satisfied with providing a model, a photograph, computer graphic or other replacement representation.

A number of researchers have produced models that identify styles of learning. Most are research models, but two generally stand out as practically applicable to trainers – the Peter Honey and Alan Mumford Learning Styles Questionnaire and David Kolb's Learning Style Inventory.

Learning Style Inventory

Kolb's Learning Style Inventory from his *Experiential Learning: Experience as a Source of Learning and Development*, (Prentice-Hall, 1984) is an instrument that many trainers find too complex and complicated to use in a practical situation, but there can be no doubt that it is invaluable as a research instrument.

The concept on which the inventory is based is quite simple, straightforward and easily understood, being a statement of what happens (or should happen) when people learn. In Kolb's concept of the learning cycle, the acquisition of new knowledge, skills and attitudes is contained in the process of 'confrontation among four modes of experiential

CONCRETE EXPERIENCE

ACTIVE
EXPERIMENTATION

REFLECTIVE
OBSERVATION

ABSTRACT
CONCEPTUALIZATION

Figure 5.1 *Kolb's Learning Cycle*

learning'. The model is shown in Figure 5.1 with the four modes labelled concrete experience, reflective observation, abstract conceptualization and active experimentation.

DESIGN APPLICATION 8

If Kolb's model is to be introduced into the training, the original works should be studied and used to introduce and describe the model.

Practical application is by means of a questionnaire which identifies strengths of preferences by scoring and translating the preferred styles by means of graphic entries.

Consideration can then be given to modification of the preferences if they are not sufficiently rounded.

The Learning Cycle

Kolb's research for his Learning Style Inventory was carried out in the United States. Somewhat similar studies were conducted in the United Kingdom by Peter Honey and Alan Mumford. However, these two management development consultants and psychologists followed a much

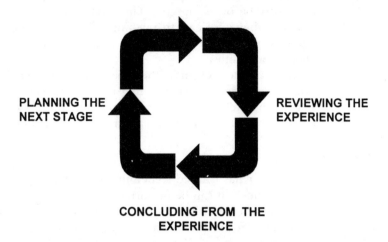

HAVING AN EXPERIENCE

PLANNING THE NEXT STAGE

REVIEWING THE EXPERIENCE

CONCLUDING FROM THE EXPERIENCE

Figure 5.2 *The relationship between the learning cycle and the Honey/Mumford learning preferences*

more pragmatic path than that of Kolb and the result, the Learning Style Questionnaire, is a more practical instrument for general and training use.

The Honey/Mumford approach is also based on the classical learning cycle, but uses less academic labels than those of Kolb. This more practical model is shown in Figure 5.2. As with Kolb, the Honey and Mumford learning cycle represents the ideal, fully effective approach to learning. This cycle 'starts' with the learner doing something, experiencing something, feeling something – whether it be factual, practical or emotional. Following the experience, learning is reinforced by a second stage, period of reflection during which the learner reflects on what has been observed during, and what can be recalled about, the experience: *what* in fact happened, *how* it happened, *who* did it, *what* the result was, and so on – all the observable incidents which can be stored as factual, detailed information. This activity requires the learner to stop any other or furthering action in order to 'catalogue' the reflections.

In the third stage, the data collected are analysed in terms of the reasons for what happened, the reasons behind the incidence, alternative ways in which the experience might have taken place, an identification of the most effective option, and many other theoretical considerations based on what was done and what was seen to be done. This is the stage of the theorist or conceptualizer.

But conceptualization has to be translated into action if it is to have any worth. This takes place in the fourth stage, the stage when the pragmatist becomes supreme. The watchword of this person is 'If it isn't practical, then it isn't worth anything.' This is when the historical considerations are translated into future, practical action by people who care about practicalities.

The cycle then returns to the experience, which may be a repeat of the original experience incorporating the lessons learned in the previous stages. The cycle recommences, hopefully with a shorter lifetime, the lessons learned on the first occasion producing a fully effective event.

Learning Preferences

The learner has learned something at all stages to the extent that an effective function can be performed. This, of course, is the ideal. Most people have a preference for one or more of these learning stages, and if these singular preferences are strong and overpowering, problems of incomplete learning arise.

For example, a learner who becomes 'locked in' on the active, doing stage is less likely to stop to reflect or analyse and consequently will repeat the original mistakes or even make new ones. The reflector who is so enamoured with considering what has happened will let life pass by with others making decisions, taking action and so on. The locked-in theorist will become so interested in the convolutions of the internal intricacies that nothing will be done. The pragmatist at the end of the cycle might destroy or ignore all that has preceded because if it is not a practical event it must be of no value or interest.

Naturally, not everybody has one preference only. The ideal must be to have a balance of all stage preferences, but in practice most people have one or two strong preferences with the others either weak or just appearing.

The Learning Style Questionnaire

Using the learning cycle as their basis, Honey and Mumford (*The Manual of Learning Style*, Peter Honey, 1982, 1986 and 1992) considered its use in relation to what managers and professional people do. Several thousand people have now been involved in their research, which has led them to the identification of four common styles of preferred learning. They constructed an instrument, the Learning Styles Questionnaire, to identify these preferred learning approaches within the learning cycle. Naturally, some individuals will have a preference and ability to learn in more than one mode, but Honey and Mumford found that most people, rather than follow the full learning cycle in a totally effective learning manner, tended to prefer one or two modes and 'lock in' on a preferred style, often to the detriment of their learning.

The four styles identified are labelled Activist, Reflector, Theorist and Pragmatist. These relate to the learning cycle as shown in Figure 5.3.

Activists

These are people who enjoy doing something, even at times just for the sake of doing it. They revel in innovations, but tend to get bored quickly and look for other interests. The Activist learner prefers experiential learning events with lots of activities, games and exercises and a minimum of input sessions. The Activist preference trainer includes many activities, questionnaires and tasks in his or her events and while the learners are performing these, can be at a loss as to what to do - ('I wish they'd get on with it?', 'Should I join in and help them?', 'Why are they taking so long' and so on.)

Reflectors

People with this preference are usually the quieter learners who, although interested in new concepts and ideas, would rather sit back and observe others taking part, extracting learning from their observations. They like to look at all angles and are cautious before making a move. If this is a very strong preference, they can be locked in to it and become very annoyed with the Activist who wants to 'get on with it'. The Reflector

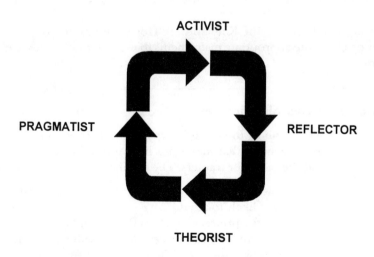

ACTIVIST

PRAGMATIST

REFLECTOR

THEORIST

Figure 5.3 *The Honey and Mumford Learning Cycle*

trainer can tend to build in too many periods to sit and think as opposed to doing.

Theorist

This type of learner must also reflect, but to a deeper extent: they insist on knowing and understanding all the principles, models and theories behind any learning ideas. The various approaches are weighed against each other and the 'best' approach analysed. They tend to think in objective, rational, logical ways and are disturbed by subjective approaches and impressions. Their attitude is 'If it can't be explained logically, I don't want to know.'

Pragmatist

The Pragmatist is an Activist keen to try out new ideas and methods, but only if these are practical and they can see a direct and specific application at work. They are essentially practical, down-to-earth people who will immerse themselves in problem-solving and decision-making events – as long as there is a real end product that can be put to good use.

DESIGN APPLICATION 9

The Learning Style Questionnaire can be issued to the learners, either before or after descriptions of the model as described above. My preference is to use the questionnaire, score the results, then discuss the implications in terms of preferences etc.

Trainers should refer to the Kolb and the Honey and Mumford references for information about the appropriate instruments to use, their rationales and areas for discussion.

Learning Style/Preference Significances

When one of these models is used in a TDP event, the learners must become aware that the results have two significances – one for learners and the other for trainers. The significances for learners include:

- how the preferences affect the learning events which they are most likely to attend
- how the preferences affect the amount of learning they achieve in an event, whether this event links with their stronger preferences or weaker ones
- that fully effective learning only occurs if they do not allow themselves to become locked in to one or two preference roles.

As far as the significance of styles for trainers is concerned, in addition to the ones listed above, the specific trainer list will also include:

- a realization of their own preferences and how these might affect the design and implementation of training events
- their relationships with learners who have either the same or opposite preference characteristics
- their behaviour during a training event.

DESIGN APPLICATION 10

When the learners have identified and discussed their own learning styles and the implications for them as learners, the significances of learning styles to them as trainers should be introduced. This can be introduced by putting the learners into sub-groups to discuss their profiles and their reaction to them, the implications of different preferences on training events, and the specific implications for their training if they decide either to modify their behaviour or stay with their preferences.

Figure 5.4 summarizes the significances and implications of learning styles and their preferences for the trainer and can be used as the basis for an input session, a discussion or as a handout linked with a session on this topic. If you have preferences for particular styles, preferences that may be interfering with your training, you may overlook some alternative activities. The final column of the table suggests modifications you might consider making.

Learning style	Preferred activities	You may overlook possibilities	Modify action
Activist	Practical games exercises and activities	Some learners prefer inputs in addition to practical events	Offer wide range of learning opportunities
	Encouraging group to be responsible for all the learning	Support by you when learning risk is high	Leading, but not directing
	Changing the programme several times	Learners may prefer a forecast progression to unforeseen change	Discuss changes with group before taking action

	Keeping the event moving all the time	Learners require opportunities to consider, reflect and consolidate	Build in reflection and and discussion periods
Reflector	Learning events with with a large amount of reflection and discussion	The event has to be kept moving, with activities	Plan varied programme with balance of activity and consideration
	Emphasis in feed-back on what happened rather than why	Learners may want to examine the event in depth	Make reviews of events wide ranging and searching
	Events which are 'quiet' and considerative	Many learners want a more lively type of event	Again, plan a varied type of programme
Theorist	Complex learning programmes with detailed examinations of theories, models and 'academic' arguments and concepts	Some learners will bored with what they consider to be overlong	Plan the reviews to a depth in line with the level and interests of the learners in mind
	A preponderance of lectures and input sessions	The need for lighter, more active sessions even though the material may still be essentially 'taught'	Vary the event to replace some of the imputs with activities that will still allow the learning to emerge

Ensure that the in-depth objectives that require a teaching approach are essential to the necessary objectives of the event and that the lecture is the only relevant and effective technique.

Pragmatist	Where the learning material is based firmly on 'real-world' material, case studies and activities	Wider aspects can be presented with constructed activities, planned to include all the learning points	Plan a balanced event which has a real-life studies as well as constructed ones on real life
	The learners are used frequently in practical activities as they are accustomed to this at work	Although real-life tend to repeat, the full circumstances may not always be the same	Use experience and experiences with the caveat that the differences are described
	There is considerable	It is often necessary	Make the planning of

emphasis on planning action on return to work to help the learning process	to include some 'fun' activities in a programme of mere mortals	future action, if not voluntary, then one in which the learner has considerable personal control

Figure 5.4 *Learning style preferences and the trainer*

People's attitude and approach to learning vary widely – as do the problems they encounter. The new trainer must be aware of this from the start, otherwise the question will be raised, 'I'm doing everything right. Why aren't they learning?' or 'They are all receiving the same training. Why are some of them not learning, even though they are as intelligent as the others?' When the significance of styles is appreciated, the answers to these questions become obvious.

6 Communication and Learning Approaches

▷   CHAPTER SUMMARY   ◁

This chapter:

- considers the problems of learning encountered in training events
- discusses the variety of learning approaches possible to enable learning to take place
- identifies the barriers to verbal communication and discusses remedies
- extends the verbal communication role by its supplementary and complementary non-verbal aspects of speech and communication
- considers the problems raised by the limited attention span of learners and listeners and suggests ways of avoiding this problem
- introduces alternative training approaches to traditional input sessions or presentations.

Problems of Learning

Communication and learning are multi-aspected and are affected by general as well as personal factors. Most of the general ones affect most learners to some degree or other and the effective trainer must be aware of them and the possible remedial actions.

One general problem is that of memory retention and recall over time of material learned. Figure 6.1 demonstrates the extent to which learning is recalled over the short period of time of one day. Beyond that, depending on other circumstances, there is a further falling off of recall which may in time reduce to zero.

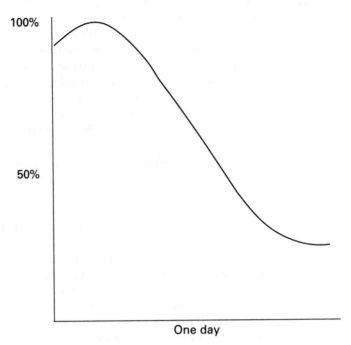

100%

50%

One day

Figure 6.1 *Learning Recall*

The amount of recall fall-away in such a short period of time is alarming, but unfortunately only too real in many cases. Naturally there will be individuals whose intrinsic recall is much greater over large periods, but equally there may be some who remember less for even shorter periods than that shown. This, of course, is not the full story, but it represents what happens on so many training occasions and happens when learning is taken for granted.

The solution to this undesirable situation is repetition of the learning at intervals designed to reinforce memory and recall powers, linked with other training approaches to support the repetition. Some of the strategies used in this process include:

- *Impact*: events, information, etc are normally remembered much more easily if something accompanies them that gives them an impact, helping the individual to consolidate the learning in their mind. This impact need not be explosive, but it should be sufficiently different from the norm to be outstanding.

- *Linked items*: a series of isolated pieces of information which have either no connection with each other or are sufficiently different,

71

even within one subject, to appear to be singular topics will make recall much more difficult. Some items will be recalled – the ones the learner is most interested in, but these may not be the ones the trainer wants to be recalled. Linking a series of facts or ideas will help the learner to associate the total information and make recall easier – an example of this linking is the memory system of making up a progressive story using the singular items to be remembered.

- *Progressive reviews*: the advice given to presenters is, 'Tell the audience what you are going to tell them; tell them: tell them what you have told them'. This is the essence of trying to ensure that your learners remember and can recall much more than the minimal amount shown in Figure 6.1. At the very least, a summary at the end of the session will help this recall. Further support can be given by a comprehensive summary at the end of the day's training. The following morning the previous day's work can be reviewed – for example, by the learners' presentations of what they have included in the previous day's learning log. If possible, and it is certainly advisable, further reminders of the learning should take place at intervals – perhaps an activity involving the learning points; a test if the learning is of an area of knowledge; a discussion for the learners to describe their views on the learning so far; and of course, an end-of-event review and formulation of action plans. Reminders of this nature are essential in ensuring that a maximum amount of learning is remembered and can be recalled. Hopefully, when the learner returns to work, implementation of the learning will act as a further, strengthening reminder.

In almost every training situation and for whatever subject, the criterion must be that the initial presentation or demonstration cannot be solely relied upon for learning recall – the learning points, preferably presented in an impactive interesting way and linked in a logical sequence or series must be followed up with reviews, ideally in a varied way, over as long a period as possible from the training event through to implementation and beyond.

Learning Approaches

Whatever form of training or learning might be involved, there are some common attributes, which relate to the human ability, or inability, to learn in particular ways. Again, these are generalizations, but ones that relate to the majority of learners.

Dale in *Educational Media* (Merrill, 1969) and supported by a wide variety of other researchers showing approximately the same amounts, proposed that memory and learning levels were strongly dependent on the manner in which the material was presented. He attributed the following percentages of recall to different learning approaches:

10 per cent of what is read
20 per cent of what is heard
30 per cent of what is seen
50 per cent of what is heard and seen
70 per cent of what is said and written
90 per cent of what is said as it is done.

The least successful in most cases is reading alone and the most successful is taking action and at the same time describing the action. This has considerable significance for the trainer who reinforces self-learning each time a subject is taught, particularly when there is an associated practical activity.

There is a Chinese proverb attributed to Confucius which is often quoted by trainers:

I hear and I forget
I see and I remember
I do and I understand.

Problems of Communication

Communication is the trainer's principal tool in helping people learn, but this medium can produce many difficulties and problems. Communication can take many forms and each has its advantages and disadvantages.

Barriers to verbal communication

Learners will use most frequently verbal communication in their training activities, whether in one-to-one face to face, or dealing with groups of varying sizes. There are many barriers facing the trainer and learners in such situations.

Rather than use an input session format to consider verbal communication and its problems with the learning group, one aspect of the many barriers can be demonstrated through using design application 11.

DESIGN APPLICATION 11

Introduce the activity by saying 'Let's have a look at one of these barriers'.

1. Ask for a volunteer, or alternatively select a learner whom you have assessed as having an 'average' level of verbal ability.
2. Give the 'volunteer' a sheet of paper that contains a drawing and instructions on what they should do – to describe the drawing verbally, without using any other aid, including hand movements, for the participants to draw the object from the description. No questions are allowed. Give the learner two or three minutes to consider the situation.
3. While the learner is digesting the task, issue sheets of acetate to the remainder of the group and water-based, acetate marker pens.
4. Tell the learner group that the 'volunteer' will have up to five minutes to describe an object which they should draw on the acetate sheets.
5. Tell them that they cannot ask any questions during the description.
6. Give the communicator up to five minutes to describe the drawing.
7. Project all the completed acetate sheets
8. Project an OHP slide of the drawing described.

An activity of this nature will probably take about 12 minutes, depending on the number of participants and the time taken to project all the acetate attempts. It should be followed by a discussion which should include the following questions:

- How difficult did you find it and why?'
- What would have made the task easier?'

The one-way communication just demonstrated and discussed represents one of the problems encountered in verbal communication. Others can be considered in 'family' groups.

Language
Vocabulary. The vocabulary and its extent must be limited to the range that the listeners can understand, otherwise you might be talking in a foreign language!

Jargon. It is very easy to pick up the jargon of the organization or the discipline, but if the listeners do not come from the same environment the jargon will not only not be understood, it will annoy.

Ambiguity. Be careful that you say what you mean, not simply what you mean to say. Extra care is essential when the audience is multicultural and words and sayings may have different meaning – or mean nothing at all.

Woolly approach and/or rambling. The advice of KISS (Keep it short and simple) must be kept in mind and the long, vague rambling speech will be avoided. Otherwise there is the danger of the audience stopping listening or even falling asleep.

Unusual words. If the words are unusual for you, ensure that you are using the best word, the right word and you are pronouncing it correctly. Are you using it because it is the best/only/correct/most appropriate word, or are you simply using it for effect? Is the audience likely to understand it?

Psychological (on the part of the listeners)

Pressures. All sorts of pressures are on members of an audience and these can detract and distract from listening fully to what is said – pressures of work, health, domestic, money, learning, etc, pressures can all have an effect.

Mood. The listener who is easily affected by the mood they are in may not be in the right mood to make listening to you a priority.

Forced resistance. Not every learner attends a training programme voluntarily and if someone has been directed to attend against their will, they are most unlikely to be in a receptive mood and will, perhaps, actively resist learning.

Fear. Fear can be a strong motivator for listening and learning, but if it is too strong, it becomes a barrier to listening and learning, the fear being uppermost in the person's mind.

Shyness. The learner has overcome the first shyness barrier by actually attending, but if something is not understood the shyness may prevent a question with the result that what follows is lost.

Aggression. This may be linked with enforced attendance, an on-the-spot dislike of you, the learning environment or the other learners, but it will usually exhibit itself by aggressive expression which is developed rather than listening to what you are saying.

Resistance to learning. The reasons for this attitude can be many – enforced attendance, failure to see the reason for the training, dislikes of a variety of nature and so on. An attitude of 'I do not intend to learn' can sometimes be overcome by involvement or an interesting presentation or activity, but often it stays throughout the session.

Know it all already. One of the common resistances to learning, particularly by the long-serving employee who has been sent on the training against their wishes. If this is indeed the case, it is more effective to try to use their experience within the group than to try to react against the attitude.

Too old to learn. This is usually an attitude developed by those who are frightened to learn or otherwise do not want to learn. Research has shown that, unless older people have allowed their minds to degenerate, they are often, because of a wealth of experience, better learners than many younger people.

Status differences. If the learners on a particular training event come from different status levels within an organization, unless the group is well-established the higher-level members may resist in case they make fools of themselves in front of their juniors, who themselves do not want to take the risk of showing themselves up in front of their bosses.

Mind not on the learning. If the learner's mind is still on what has been left at work, or has other worries such as moving house, being responsible for making arrangements for a variety of events, has an interview looming and so on, full attention will not be paid to the learning.

Environment

Noise, heat, cold, ventilation, space available. These are all aspects of the physical environment which can get in the way of listening and learning. Sometimes they can be resolved, at other times nothing can be done and they may remain as barriers.

Interruptions/work intrusion. Interruptions, of whatever nature but particularly if they bring work into the learning environment, will affect listening and learning. Most can be avoided by preliminary precautions.

Restricted time. Learning requires adequate time to be effective – time to fit in the material of the event; time for different learners to assimilate material; time for the trainer to put over the material effectively; and so on. If there is a time restriction, this will have a detrimental effect on both the trainer and learner.

Speech

Unskilled speaker. An unskilled speaker will use methods and techniques which are not the most effective in having an impact on the listeners. Too many hesitations, verbal noises, mannerisms and so on will be noted by the listeners who may take more notice of these than of what is being said. There may be an element of sympathy for the inexperienced speaker, but lack of skill is unlikely to be approved.

Accent. At one time regional accents were not acceptable for many areas of public speaking. This has now been discounted, but if the accent is too strong, it may not be understandable. The use of dialect words, however, should be avoided as these may not be widely understood.

Manner. Speakers may not be able to completely control their inherent manner, but usually this can be modified somewhat for the period required. A patronizing manner is soon recognized and rejected by the listeners; aggression from the speaker results in either withdrawal or returned aggression, neither of which are conducive to good communication; an abrasive manner has a similar effect. Speakers can usually modify the first two; the last one is more difficult as the speaker may not even be aware of this aspect of their natural manner.

Attitude. This is often an aspect of which the speaker is aware but which nevertheless may have an effect on the extent of listening and acceptance. The speaker's *prejudices* may emerge unconsciously – racism, sexism and so on, and personal views which ignore or reject the views of others without reason or argument. The speaker may be *judgemental,* making decisions or forcing opinions without seeking other options and, perhaps because of these two aspects and other internal motivation, may be *over-directive.* Trainers have to be completely aware of these possible attitudes in themselves and, if present, modify their approaches accordingly. Changing an over-directive approach is particularly important in training with more and more emphasis being placed on learner-centred rather than trainer-centred control.

The know-it-all. The speaker may be an expert on the subject and may in fact know 'all' there is to know about it, but listeners are very easily turned-off by someone who ensures that they become aware of this extent of knowledge.

Lack of knowledge. The converse of knowing it all and letting everybody be aware of this, is the speaker whose knowledge of the subject is limited or incomplete. The listener, particularly in a learning situation, has every justification in rejecting someone who has obviously not taken sufficient care to ensure that they know their subject. Naturally not everybody knows everything and at times the trainer will admit some lack of knowledge, making a firm promise to find out. But if this becomes an over-frequent admission, credibility will soon be lost.

The Elements of Communication

Communication can be considered in three aspects:

- verbal communication
- non-verbal aspects of speech
- non-verbal communication.

Verbal communication will be considered in detail later when presentation skills for trainers are discussed. Verbal communication is always supplemented and complemented by various forms of non-verbal communication.

Non-verbal Aspects of Speech

Non-verbal aspects of speech include the mannerisms or noises designed to demonstrate interest, listening and continuity. These are the 'er', 'hmm', 'uh-huh' and others that most people use. Used deliberately but not too frequently, they can encourage a speaker; used excessively, they can annoy the other person.

Non-verbal Communication

Non-verbal communication (NVC) includes the body signals we employ – whether or not we are aware of them, and to which we react, again sometimes subconsciously. Research has shown that of these three aspects, non-verbal communication usually takes on more significance than the spoken word, particularly if the two are not congruent. Various researches suggest that NVC represents between 70 and 80 per cent of our messages that get through to others, compared with 10 to 20 per cent of verbal communication.

There are three principal options for presenting aspects of NVC on a trainer development programme – the one you use will depend on the time available for this part of communication sessions. These options are given in design applications 12 to 14, with a follow-up activity to be used after whichever type of session is chosen, in design application 15.

DESIGN APPLICATION 12

Deliver an input session, with discussion, on the various aspects of NVC in such areas as:

Arm barriers	Hand gestures
Hand-to-face gestures	Head gestures
Handshaking	Eye signals
Facial gestures	Postures
Sitting and sitting postures	Proxemic zones
Clusters of behaviour	

Complete material for a session of this nature can be found in a range of publications including *The Psychology of Interpersonal Behaviour*, Michael Argyle, Penguin, 1967; *How to Read a Person Like a Book*, Nierenberg and Colero, Thorsons, 1980. The subject is also included as chapters or sections of a number of other publications including *The Techniques of Training*, Leslie Rae, Gower, 1993.

DESIGN APPLICATION 13

A second approach might include an input session using the selected range of material in summary form, the comments being supplemented and complemented by a relevant video.

There are a number of appropriate videos available, but I would recommend *Body Language*. Allan Pease, Connaught Training 1987 and *Silent Signals*. Allan Pease. Connaught Training 1989.

DESIGN APPLICATION 14

The third approach in this range, particularly if time is limited or needs to be strongly controlled, uses the video alone, followed by a detailed discussion on the subject, the discussion time limited by the time available.

DESIGN APPLICATION 15

Whichever method is used to introduce the subject, it must be followed by a sub-group activity asking the learners to discuss NVC and its significance to them as trainers, how they can use it and any problems they envisage. This activity should be reviewed in the full learning group and conclusions summarized on a flipchart and posted.

The information about non-verbal communication can be reinforced by the use of a relevant activity which enables non-verbal communication to be practised, observed and commented on. A number of activities of this nature are included in activity source books and generally are performed using a 'goldfish bowl' technique. In these cases it is helpful if a simple form of NVC behaviour analysis is introduced and used by the observing groups.

The Learning Attention Span

No trainer training on communication and learning would be complete without some comments on how the learners are seeing what is being presented to them. There is a finite time during which learners will listen to a presentation with full attention. Research suggests that in the majority of cases this is about 20 minutes. After this presentation period, attention starts to stray and reduce, usually only to return a short while before the known end of the session - the learners anticipate the end of the session and come to life.

A useful rule-of-thumb when you are presenting session material is to talk for no longer than (and often for less than) 20 minutes before changing the tempo of the session. At this stage, a sub-group discussion or task-solving activity can be introduced to reduce the passivity of the learners. For instance a video might be shown, with the learners being told that a related activity will follow it. Impact events should occur throughout the session at relevant points; the longer the session, the more impactive the events. But the principal criterion is that a change must be introduced which will break the inevitable pattern of reducing attention.

Alternative Training Approaches

Still the most common training approach is the input session, presentation or lecture during which the trainer presents information and facts about the subject of the session. This, as a singular approach, is probably, in most cases, the least effective form of encouraging learning, although it has its place in the overall scheme of training. However, bearing in mind the necessity for variation within a session and a learning programme, the trainer who is to be as effective as possible must be aware of and skilled in other training techniques, approaches and methods. Some of these can form separate sessions within a trainer development programme, but awareness at an early stage in the programme is to be recommended.

A list of such strategies will include the following and can be presented to the learners. Or the learners can be placed in sub-groups to identify the strategies themselves and present their views.

- *Activities/Exercises/Games* – events in which the learners take part in real or constructed practical activities which involve their working together to solve problems, make decisions and so on
- *Brainstorming* – a wide-ranging and free group discussion to produce a mass of ideas
- *Buzz groups* – groups of two or more people who discuss a subject for a short time without leaving the room. This is ideal to encourage people to talk together in the early stages of an event
- *Case studies* – real or manufactured complex problems analysed in detail by groups to provide solutions

- *Demonstrations* – the trainer or trainee performs an operation or skill while the learners observe
- *Discussions* – a controlled discussion during which the learners discuss a subject to produce ideas, information or solutions
- *Open learning* – sometimes referred to as 'distance learning'. The use by the learner, usually at work, sometimes at home rather than on a training course, of learning packages which can contain a mixture of text material, videos, computer programs and so on. Can be supported by a centrally located trainer or unsupported
- *Practicals* – activities in which the learners carry out a task or process, rather than sit more passively in an input session
- *Programmed learning* – a text for the learner with a series of questions or tasks which must be completed before continuing to the next stage
- *Projects* – exercises restricted in time and extent in gathering information, performance of a task or the production of materials
- *Question and answer* – a session or period during which the trainer poses questions to the group for responses
- *Reading* – learning from a book, article or handout, during the training or away from it
- *Role plays* – any activity, usually with two participants, in which the learners are given roles, real or artificial, to carry out realistically or dramatically
- *Seminars* – usually defined as meetings or group discussions of a series of related topics
- *Simulations* – the duplication as far as possible of a real situation as a complex problem or activity with the learners taking on roles or positions
- *Syndicates/sub-groups* – learners are formed into small groups given either identical or different tasks to perform. The views are then presented to the other groups in a plenary session
- *Videos* – the viewing by learners of a pre-prepared video (commercial or internally-produced) followed by a discussion or review.

Including a variety of approaches

Common approaches to identifying the reasons why effective trainers use a variety of training techniques, are either the trainer presenting the reasons, or, preferably, the learners identifying and discussing them, first in sub-groups then in the full learner group. Whichever method is used, the final list should include:

- all parts of the learning cycle
- changing pace
- energizers
- everybody involved
- group responsibility
- ice breakers
- introducing activity to counter passivity
- mixing groups
- motivators
- quick impact (short activities)
- reinforcing input learning points
- replacing input to show learning points
- team building
- validating learning.

7 Presentation Skills

▷   CHAPTER SUMMARY   ◁

This chapter:

- describes the first week 10-minute presentation and the pre-course action
- summarizes the presentational skills support sessions
- describes in detail three methods of planning a session and producing a brief
- describes the first week 20-minute presentation
- describes the second week multi-trainer presentation.

Introduction

Guidance in presentation skills and, even more so, practice in the 'safe' environment of the training event are essential in a trainer development programme. It is here that the learner can experiment in relative safety from ridicule with 'new' presentation techniques and receive honest feedback on their performances.

TDPs cannot have too much presentation practice, in fact, because of the limited time available on most events, too little time is usually available. I recommend two formal presentations in the first of the two weeks, and one in the second. In addition to these there are, of course, the more informal ones on such aspects as learning logs, personal objectives, sub-group report-backs on an individual basis, visual aid presentations, etc if these activities are included. But in a two-week programme, there must be time for:

- one 10-minute talk early in the programme
- one 20-minute presentation during the first week
- one multi-trainer presentation during the second week.

Advice to Learners Prior to the Programme

If the learners are asked to perform certain activities prior to attending the programme, this will:

- save preparation time during the event
- prepare the learners with advance training information
- set the scene for the learners to learn on the programme.

When the two-week programme is followed, with the three specific presentations described above included, the learners should be expected to perform some preparation before attending the first week for the initial 10-minute presentation and for the later 20-minute presentation.

The 10-minute Presentation

This presentation should preferably take place on the second day of the first week, to help the learners to become accustomed to presenting sessions and to give initial feedback. The level of the presentation will also give the trainers an indication of the skill levels of the learners.

Pre-course preparation

With the first workshop joining instructions sent to the learners, or as a separate communication, the learners should be advised that they will be expected to present a 10-minute session during the workshop. The subject will be their own choice from a list of subjects proposed by the TDP trainers – I have used training topics as this supports the learning process of the programme. The list can include:

- establishing training needs
- identifying training needs
- questioning techniques in training
- the use of the lecture or input session
- the use of syndicates in training
- discussion leading
- the construction and use of visual aids
- the design and use of handouts
- videos in training
- games, activities and simulation
- any other subjects the trainers or the learners themselves wish to include.

The learners should:

- Read selected chapters from an appropriate general, descriptive training book, eg, *The Techniques of Training*, Leslie Rae, (Gower, 1993) to give them an introduction to training methods and techniques and to give them material on which to base their 10-minute presentation. They should also discuss the subject with an experienced trainer, if one is available
- Select a topic from the list
- Notify the trainers of their choice (with a second choice) prior to the session. (The trainers responsible for the session should ensure that there is not too much duplication of subjects and notify the learners if they need to change their chosen subject)
- Make notes, script or brief in preparation for their presentation of their chosen topic
- Decide whether to use any training aids (audio or visual), notify the trainers of their requirements and produce whatever they intend to use.

Advice should be given that the material will not be expected to cover the full subject and the learners should base their presentation on the most effective use of the 10 minutes.

Presentation Practice

As suggested above, a useful time for the learners to make their 10-minute presentation is during the afternoon of the second day. If the full learning group numbers 10 to 12, it should be divided into two sub-groups which will operate separately for this stage, each under the direction of a trainer.

Time should be given for them to complete their preparation for the presentations, and the trainers should be available for guidance, advice and assistance during this preparation. As the learners should have prepared their presentation prior to the training programme, this time should be limited (say, 15 minutes).

The learners should be allocated a running order for the presentations, or have them arrange this themselves, and the presentations run under the control of the trainer on this occasion. The time limit of 10 minutes for each presentation should be strictly enforced as this is part of a session preparation and performance technique.

Following each presentation, the trainer should lead a review and feedback session. This could follow the lines of asking the presenter first for self-review, then asking the audience group for comments, with the trainer summarizing the review and adding significant points which may have been omitted. This review should not be heavy or over-critical and could usefully concentrate on whether the presentation had a clear start, main body and conclusion; the effectiveness (and relevance) of any aids; and asking the presenter what changes (if any) they would make if they were to repeat the presentation.

After the review and feedback session, the learners should be given some time (say 15 minutes) to reflect on their performances and on the feedback received, and to make personal notes (in their learning logs) about improvement actions for future reference.

Presentational Skills Support Sessions

Prior to the major 20-minute presentation during the first week, it is necessary to offer input sessions/discussions/activities related to the skills used in presentations: session design and planning; script construction; the construction and use of visual aids; verbal presentation techniques. Whichever sessions are included, the basic criteria should be followed – minimum input by the trainer, maximum participation by the learners.

A number of support sessions should precede the principal 20-minute presentations in order to give the learners the maximum help for this area of work, an area that is usually so important for trainers, particularly new ones. These sessions can cover:

- CCTV and video in training
- environment preparation
- listening skills
- observation and feedback skills
- presentational skills – verbal and non-verbal
- questioning skills
- role plays
- script or brief preparation
- technology
- the design, production and use of visual aids
- the use of activities, etc.

Obviously to precede presentation practice with all these topics would result in overkill, so significant subjects have to be selected. The ones I have used successfully have included:

- environment preparation
- presentational skills – verbal and non-verbal
- questioning skills
- script or brief preparation
- the design, production and use of visual aids.

There is insufficient space in this guide to comment in detail all these aspects, but you will find several publications that give specific guidance in the recommended reading list at the end of this book. Guidance on the activities to precede the presentations will be of particular interest at this stage, especially the preparation of the session brief or script.

Script or Brief Preparation

There are few trainers, experienced or not, who perform their training without any form of script or brief. New trainers should be recommended to have this essential document with them at all times during their session. It may be that new trainers are given a brief with which to present the sessions for which they are made responsible, but even this should eventually be personalized when the new trainer becomes more comfortable with the role. A knowledge of brief construction will enable modifications to be made more easily and effectively.

There are three principal methods of producing scripts:

- using the traditional method to plan and make notes
- using the headline method of producing a brief
- using horizontal planning to plan and use a brief.

The Traditional, Vertical Method of Session Planning

This is the full-script method, and although it should not be used during the actual session, it has a valuable place when designing a session and writing the initial brief from which a working brief can be made.

Writing out text in full
In this case the text of the script or brief is written out in full, word for word as if it were a report or essay. The wording should preferably be in the style of the 'spoken' word rather than the 'written' word, using 'can't' rather than 'cannot' and so on.

Division into paras and sub-paras
It is helpful to divide the script into paragraphs and sub-paragraphs, each with their headlines, not just for any grammatical or appearance reasons, but to make the different parts of the text clearer visually. Different

colours can be used for alternate paragraphs (or sections) and if the brief is produced on a computer, different fonts can be used to aid this purpose.

Underlining for emphasis

One of the necessary actions to be taken with a script of this nature, is to make the different parts as separate and as visually impactive as possible. Underlining, either single or double can be used, particularly **with bold printing** if this is available.

Colours for emphasis

Bold and different colours can be used as another method for producing emphasis in the document. These can be produced by the use of coloured pens if the script is hand-written, or coloured print if typewritten or word processed. In the latter cases, if monocolour only is available, colour can be added by the use of highlighter pens.

Framing for emphasis or isolation

Adding a frame or boxed border, particularly if combined with some or all of the previously described emphasis producers, can have added impact and be attention-grabbing. Remember, however, that if too much use is made of any one effect, the impact is lost.

Leaving broad margins

It is helpful to leave broader than normal borders on both sides of the text so that notes can be added – comments made during the session, amendments that become necessary as a result of session comments, directions to reconsider certain aspects and so on, in addition to stage directions such as those described in the next section.

Leave plenty of space between paragraphs or sections to isolate them or make the differences more apparent.

Stage directions

These are used for OHPs, handouts, questions and timings. The margins can be used to make stage direction entries such as:

- when to use which training aid – OHP, flipchart, audio cassette, video and so on
- when to issue a named or numbered handout
- the occasion to ask a question
- the occasion to break the group into sub-groups for an activity and so on.

Timings can also be included at stages throughout the text. Do not write actual times – after all the session may not start at the advertised time and therefore any time will be wrong. Rather, enter the period of time by which the stage in the script should have been reached. If the session is divided into very definite sections, an alternative might be a time period for each section of the workshops.

Headline Planning

This technique is an abbreviation of the traditional full-script method of preparing a brief and involves cutting out many of the words in the full script and using a shorthand form only. The method is as follows.

List headlines on A4 sheet

Identify the main subjects of the topic and list these as main subject headings. Write them down as you think of them; a logical order can be imposed later.

Enter inter-heading summarized notes

Under each main subject heading, in logical order, enter brief, summary notes of the material you would wish to include under the heading. This will not be the final note as the material will need to be edited for essential content only.

Transfer to clear sheets or index cards

When the notes have been completed – main subject headings and the contents of each section – transfer these notes to the format you will be using in the session itself. This might be sheets of A4 paper or index cards. The A4 sheets, which would normally rest on the trainer's desk or table, should be written in large enough print (not script) to be seen when the trainer is standing beside the table as well as when he or she is seated.

Index cards can be completed with rather smaller print, but this must still be sufficiently clear and large to be easily readable from, for example, a standing position near the table.

Complete brief with impact techniques

A working brief will be difficult to use if all the entries are the same. Full use of mixed print (upper and lower case), colour, underlining, boxes, highlighting, margin stage directions and so on should be made. The impact guides should be entered at this stage rather than when the content is being entered – at this stage it is easier to see where impact guides need to be placed. Err on the side of too few rather than too many as the latter can confuse, especially when you are quickly trying to find your place in the middle of a session.

Number and tag each sheet or card

Ensure that page numbers are entered on each sheet or card and punch a hole in the top, left corner of the sheet or card so that a tag can be inserted, holding the sheets together. It is only too easy to drop the set in the middle of a session with disastrous consequences if the sheets are not held together.

Horizontal Planning

This is a method that breaks away from the traditional approach and produces a document, usually on one sheet of paper, which can be used both in the planning process and as a headline brief. The planning is in four stages.

Stage 1

The first decisions the trainer has to make are concerned with the main subject areas for the presentation. When the first thoughts on these are considered, they should be entered, preferably as single words, across a sheet of paper placed in the landscape position.

DESIGN APPLICATION 16

The method can be demonstrated as it is explained to the learning group. One example that can be used is that of moving house to another town to produce a plan for a session on this subject.

The learners would be asked to suggest the main subject areas which would then be entered on a flipchart, fixed in landscape form rather than vertically, to simulate a planning A4 or larger personal sheet.

These words, or subject headings, need not be complete nor need they necessarily be in order, although this helps in the planning. But other headings may be added as the planning progresses and the brief planning may suggest a different order from the one originally considered.

Stage 2

The second stage involves considering each subject heading and noting beneath it words or phrases describing the aspects relating to that subject. For example, in the case used, under the heading 'Type of house' might appear the entries: detached, semi-detached, town house, bungalow, cottage; number of bedrooms; large, medium, small or no garden; garage, car port, etc.

DESIGN APPLICATION 17

The learning group can then suggest the sub-headings to be inserted below the main headings retained on the flipchart.

Sub-headings continue to be added until no more can be thought of at that time – others can be added later if necessary.

Stage 3
Here, the stage directions are added. If OHP slides are to be used or handouts issued, a note can be made to this effect.

Priority inclusions can be annotated. Session material can be considered at three priority levels – *must knows, should knows* and *could knows.* The first sort are essential to the session and the timing must allow for their total inclusion. The *should knows* are also important, but may be reduced if time is restricted. The *could knows* are items which, although relevant to the session, can be omitted if there is insufficient time; for example, if questioning by the learners has taken up too much time, or additional explanations have had to be given. To save space, these priority entries can be abbreviated to M, S and C. Linked with the prioritization can be estimates of the timing for the main sections. More detailed timing can be included in the working brief.

The variety of horizontal plans is wide – colours can be used for emphasis; certain important items can be enclosed in a frame or block; different sized lettering can be used, again for importance. Lines with arrows can be added to show how items need to be moved for the final version, and so on.

Stage 4
Finally, a fair copy of the plan can be produced, with material reorganized as necessary and the entries made clear. This copy can then be used to produce a more traditional script and brief, or used as it stands. If used as the brief, the stage directions may need to be supplemented or clarified.

Of course, as only headlines are included, the trainer must have a complete awareness of what needs to be said about each item, but the format has the decided advantage that the brief for one session can be contained on one, or at the most two, sheets of paper. This is most helpful when locating your place in the brief during a session. It also offers the advantage that, at a glance, the remaining material can be seen, or the order can be changed without moving pages about.

DESIGN APPLICATION 18

When the horizontal planning method has been described and questioning shows that the learners understand its principles and practical aspects, they can be asked to produce a horizontal plan. A useful subject which they can use as individuals is the subject they are to use for their 20-minute presentation. In this way the method is practised and a start is made on their actual presentation preparation.

The next major recommendation to new trainers should concern the use of briefs, particularly those in full script form. In their early days, it is certainly important that they have a full script of their session, but it is equally important that they should not use this to read from during the session. In fact, to have a full script at the session is dangerous as its presence might tempt the new trainer to simply read it out, which is likely to have the following effects:

- The learners feel that they might as well read the text themselves
- Written material read out usually sounds boring unless the reader is a skilled actor
- Eye contact would be lost with the group
- Non-verbal signals given by the group go unnoticed
- The reader's place in the script could easily be lost if they were interrupted with questions, had to use a visual aid etc.

The 20-minute Presentation

Pre-course Preparation

This practice presentation is more important than the earlier 10-minute one and will be found frightening by the majority of the learners. Consequently the trainers must be prepared to offer maximum support. In the pre-course material sent to the learners, they should be told that they will be required to make a 20-minute presentation. The presentation subject will be a completely free choice for them – work-related, non-work-related, a hobby or interest and so on. They should be advised to gather material that might be used as presentation aids – OHP slides, objects, etc, and to make some brief notes on the content of the presentation. However, they should be told not to produce a final brief, as time will be given to them on the programme to prepare fully following the support sessions on design, preparation, visual aids and so on.

Pre-practice Preparation

Allow sufficient time for the learners to plan and prepare for their presentation, write a usable script and prepare session aids – visual or audio-visual, depending on the subjects and facilities available. For the 20-minute session at least four hours should be made available for this preparation work, preferably arranged so that this is session time which can be extended into the learners' own time for final work.

Recommend that when the script is almost ready, the learner should rehearse the presentation, preferably with the aid of an audio recorder.

During the preparation time within the session, and beyond, the trainers should be available for advice and guidance, suggestions on script content, format and the preparation of aids. The maximum amount of aids should be available for the learners, duplicated as far as possible for multiple use.

The order of running should be decided at this stage, either determined by the trainers or it may be suggested to the learners that they produce their own running order and organization of the series of presentations. If the learning group is 10 or 12 in size, two separate groups, which will remain parallel, should be formed, each with a supporting trainer. The groups should be advised that:

- the presentations should last 20 minutes
- a period of 20 minutes should be allowed for review following the presentation
- the learners will be responsible for arranging the feedback (at this stage in the programme the learners may not have received guidance in observation and feedback, so some advice should be given by the trainers and they should assist in the actual feedback)
- time should be included for delays between one presenter to the next.

Practice Presentations

During the practice presentations the trainer takes a background position, yet still ready to help, advise, guide and if necessary regain order within a group. The presenter should be responsible for everything connected with the presentation – setting-up the room, obtaining the necessary aid equipment, calling the 'audience' together, starting on time and finishing within the allocated period.

Closed-circuit TV should be used, if available, although it must be recognized that its use will increase the review time. If CCTV is used, there are a number of ways it can be used in review and feedback; these are given below.

Post-presentation Reviews

Full and honest reviews following the presentations should be encouraged, preferably with the presenter him or herself starting the critique, followed by any specified observers in the audience group with any *additional* comments coming from the remainder of the group. Finally, the trainer should summarize the feedback, clarify any contradictions and certainly point out any effective approaches used which may have been ignored. As this will probably be only the learners' second presentation within the programme, the review and feedback should be handled carefully and kept at a reasonably light level, although ensuring that critical comments are made where necessary.

Use of CCTV for review purposes
Although the use of CCTV has disadvantages – it is time-consuming in reviews; it can lead to additional nervousness in the presenters; there can be problems over equipment and operation required, etc – it has a number of significant advantages. Chief among these is that the learners can, at their leisure, view themselves on video and recognize incidents to which reference might have been made. This can be most salutary. But, if CCTV is used, the video must be used in some way as part of the review and feedback. Its use certainly involves additional time during normal reviews, there are a number of alternative approaches:

1. Immediately following the presentation, the video can be used to support the normal comments by the presenter and the other members of the group. During the session, the trainer will need to have noted critical incidents and the point on the video counter at which they occur. During the review, these critical points can be re-run, rather than having to view the complete recording. There are obviously a number of variations on this approach.
2. During the next presentation, the first presenter can be excused participation so that his or her video can be viewed in private. At a later stage, this presenter can return for further audience comments. It is advisable that when this approach is used, immediately after the presentation there is some key, immediate feedback, particularly raising points the presenter should be looking for when watching the playback.
3. Verbal feedback on critical points can take place immediately after the presentation, but the presenter could take away the video to be

viewed during the evening. Post-presentation viewing can even be after the training event itself, at the presenters' workplace or in their own homes, retaining the video as a permanent reminder.

The Second Week Multi-trainer Presentation

The purpose of this multi-trainer or team presentation during the second week of the two-week TDP is to provide the learners not only with another opportunity for making a presentation about which they will receive feedback, but also to give them practice in designing and presenting a session with other trainers.

DESIGN APPLICATION 19

At the start of the second week the learners should be informed that:

- They will be fully responsible for mounting a one and a half to two hours (maximum) team presentation session on the fourth day of the week. The learning group will be divided into three sub-groups, each of which will take their turn in presenting, acting as a feedback groups and also acting as an audience for a presentation session.
- Each group will be responsible for deciding the subject for their team session, but this subject should be concerned with either training skills or organizational matters, and the presentation parts must hang together.
- All facilities and resources possible will be made available to the presenting group and the trainers will be available for advice and guidance.
- All the members of the sub-group should be involved in the presentation session(s) and a range of presentation skills, techniques and approaches will be sought.
- The learners are responsible for determining the composition of each sub-group, the timings and order of the presentations.
- One of the groups other than the one involved in the presentations will be responsible for giving feedback immediately following the presentations – how they manage this will be their responsibility. The third group will act as the audience, augmented by the trainers.

At the end of each feedback session, a trainer will give a brief feedback on the feedback group and any other significant comments. Each member of the feedback group should be involved in the feedback.

Teams should be reminded that although they are likely to concentrate most on their presentations, they should take some time considering how they will perform their feedback in the most effective manner.

The Presentations

The probable timings for the session should be posted for the information of the trainers and the learners. Assuming three teams and coffee breaks, the probable timings assume an average one and three-quarter hours presentation and an average 40 minutes feedback session, with a further 15 minutes feedback by the trainer. Teams should be warned against exceeding their time limit, to be fair to the following teams. The timetable could look like this:

Team 1

Presentation to Team 2 as audience	9.15 to 11.00
Feedback by Team 3	11.15 to 11.55
Trainer feedback	11.55 to 12.10

Team 2

Presentation to Team 3 as audience	1.15 to 3.00
Feedback by Team 1	3.00 to 3.40
Trainer feedback	3.40 to 3.55

Team 3

Presentation to Team 1 as audience	4.00 to 5.45
Feedback by Team 2	5.45 to 6.25
Trainer feedback	6.25 to 6.40
Plenary session	6.40 to 7.00

Some groups feel that to have teams of three or sometimes four, is unrealistic and never happens in their work environment. If this is the case, there is no reason not to divide the full group into pairs, a much more common team-working arrangement for trainers. This will require a major revision of timing, but on the occasions that I have arranged the presentations in this way, they have been successful and welcomed.

8 The Training Environment

▷   CHAPTER SUMMARY   ◁

This chapter:

- extends the skills and activities necessary to present an effective training session
- describes the actions required of the trainer with regard to the training environment

Introduction

In the previous section when the learner presentations were being discussed, the responsibility of the trainer for setting-up the training room or area was mentioned. This is reflected in the real life situation in which the trainer has powers to a greater or lesser degree.

Similar comments relate to the trainer's skills in designing, producing and using training aids (including visual aids) and to the range of techniques available for presenting yourself in front of the learning group.

This chapter covers the first of these three topics, albeit not in complete detail, but as mentioned previously, the recommended reading list will lead you to specific guides to the topics.

The Training Environment

The performance of training, as with any other task, can only be effective if preceded by considerable planning, design and preparation. The physical aspects of the environment in which the training is to be held are almost as important as actual skills of presentation, for if these are wrong, even the best training can fail. This aspect of training can be approached from two different levels, depending on the actual practices allowed to the trainer. Some trainers will need to develop the event from the beginning, others will have many aspects arranged by, for example, their administration section, while others will have no responsibility or authority in the matter.

The Training Room

One preparation aspect usually (although not always) open to all the classes of trainer will be the arrangement of the training room. Even when the training event has been in operation for some time, this aspect of preparation is still open to change. Of course, there are training environments which cannot be changed in any way, either because of physical constraints or organizational policy, but there are few where some minor changes cannot be made.

DESIGN APPLICATION 20

The actual training situation can be used in a practical activity to demonstrate some aspects of the training room layout.

- Divide the learners into sub-groups and ask them to consider the present layout of the training room. (If this activity is located early in a training day, the training room can have been rearranged so that it is far from ideal.)
- When the learners have had the opportunity to discuss and agree suggestions for a more appropriate arrangement – the sub-groups will need to get together to agree this – they should be asked to implement their agreed arrangement.
- When this has been done, a discussion can be held on why the arrangement was decided, what factors were taken into account and what barriers exist to producing the ideal arrangement.

Other Environmental Factors

There will obviously be other factors than seating which can have an effect on the effectiveness of the training. The trainer must take into account as many of these as are relevant during the preparation period.

DESIGN APPLICATION 21

A useful practical activity at this stage can be to have the learners, in sub-groups, identify and list the other environmental factors that might have an effect on a training event. The results could then be discussed in full session.

Barriers to Training Environment Effectiveness

Factors which might work against effectiveness will include:

- too large and 'grand' a room
- too small a room for division of the group into sub-groups
- inaccessibility of the training location for all learners
- failure to inform security of visiting learners and guest speakers.

In addition you must ensure that hygiene factors are satisfied:

- a suitable provision for notetaking facilities relevant to the particular training
- a visible clock
- administrative arrangements
- air conditioning
- arrangements for urgent messages to be relayed
- comfortable seating
- fan noise
- natural lighting
- nearby provision of telephones
- provision of paper and pens
- provision of refreshments and the times for these confirmed
- temperature control
- toilet availability
- visual aid equipment where necessary.

Also ensure other facilities are available and/or satisfactory:

- doors that open and shut and which, preferably, do not have glass panels through which outsiders can be seen (and see)
- location and suitability of electric points
- the shape of the room and its relevance to seating and training techniques
- windows which can be opened (or closed) and which can be shielded against glare.

Requirements will vary with different training locations, so ensure that you and any support you may have possess a complete and up-to-date checklist of items to be included in the preparation for the training event. An example of such a checklist can be found in *The Trainer Development Manual* (Rae, 1994), but the construction of your own is a simple but worthwhile task. The first few possible entries are shown below.

Training Environment Checklist

This checklist is intended as a guide only; omit any items which are not relevant to your actions and add any others which have been omitted.

ENVIRONMENTAL CHECK
Training room booked ....
Syndicate rooms booked ....
Access method ....
etc.

EQUIPMENT
Audio recorder and tapes ....
Video recorder, monitor and tapes ....
Video camera, camcorder, mixer, tapes ....
etc.

MATERIALS
Nameplates ....
Blotter pads ....
Small felt tip pens or similar ....
Large felt tip pens or similar ....
Drymarker pens ....
etc.

IMMEDIATELY BEFORE TRAINING EVENT
Check all seating, tables, extra seating available. ....
Check all other rooms available ....
Check equipment available and working ....
Check refreshments – water and
other supplies available ....
etc.

A Guide to Training Room Seating Arrangements

Training rooms can be arranged in a variety of ways and the ideal arrangement will obviously depend on the circumstances – the type of room, the seating available, the number of participants, the style of training and so on. Some of the possible arrangements with their advantages and disadvantages are discussed in the following paragraphs.

The Theatre or Classroom

When numbers are large, the traditional seating arrangement is the theatre or classroom style, in which chairs are placed in rows. The trainer is seated at a table at the front of the rows of seats, perhaps at a considerable distance from the furthest row.

This arrangement has the advantage that the maximum number of people can be accommodated – but that is about the sole advantage.

The Herringbone

This variation of the theatre or classroom arrangement improves somewhat the visibility between members. The rows of seats, instead of being carefully arranged so that everybody looks straight forward and the rows are parallel to the front of the room, are in rows which are diagonally inclined. The outside of a row is nearer the front than the centre, thus producing an arrow shape pointing away from the front.

The Boardroom

This is the traditional arrangement for small to medium sized groups, one in which the members sit round the outside of a large table or number of tables placed together, with the trainer at the 'head' of the table (a rectangular configuration will have two 'heads', but one will, often by tradition, be recognized as the trainer's seat).

The Open Boardroom

The open boardroom seating arrangement is similar to the traditional boardroom, but instead of the table being solid, the constituent tables are moved outwards so that a well exists within the rectangle. Other learners are able to sit in this well, thus increasing the size of the membership with only a small increase in floorspace.

The U-shape

This is a layout in the shape of a U which can be used with or without tables in front of the learners, depending on whether there will be a lot of writing and reference to papers, or whether the training will be mainly verbal or activity-based. The base of the U can be either rounded or squared-off. If tables are used, the members sit round the outside of the tables, rather like the boardroom layout, and again like the boardroom, if more members have to be accommodated they can sit at the inner sides of the tables, along the longer sides at least.

The V-shape

This is a natural development of the U shape, to try to avoid the remaining problems of visibility. The seats are arranged in the form of a V rather than a U.

The Circle

As the name suggests, the seats in this arrangement are in a circle facing towards the centre.

Clusters

Another informal and non-traditional form of seating places the members at small tables which are separated from each other and placed in different parts of the room. The tables need not be geometrically placed, some degree of inclination to each other and the part of the room where the trainer is located being possible. But the tables must be placed so that the narrow end of a rectangular table points in a forward direction. The members sit along the longer sides of the table and the short end which is facing forwards.

DESIGN APPLICATION 22

When the basic designs have been decribed briefly, the learners should be asked in sub-groups to:

- suggest other possible arrangements
- describe the advantages of each arrangement
- describe the disadvantage of each arrangement.

A summarized flipchart list can be produced from the feedback and discussion following the sub-groups activity.

Figure 8.1 *A suggested training room layout*

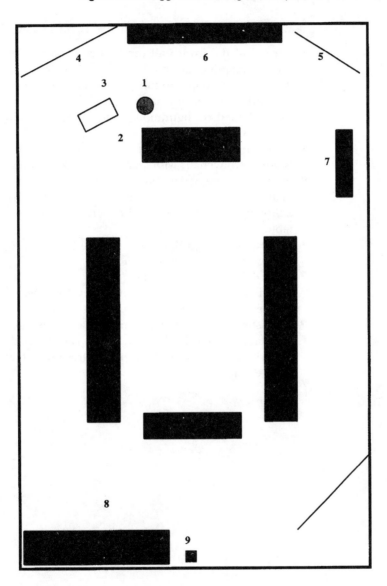

1 = Trainer   2 = Desk for script, handouts, video (when in use)
3 = OHP   4 = Screen   5 = Flipchart
6 = Wallmounted whiteboard(s)
7 = Table for refreshments, etc
8 = Tables for materials, exhibits, etc   9 = Clock

A Suggested Training Room Layout

The advantages of the layout shown in Figure 8.1 include the following:

- full use of the front wall can be made, particularly if there is a system of equipment tracks
- it is relatively simple to move from the trainer position to either the whiteboard or flipchart
- the U-shaped configuration of the learners' seating affords reasonable visibility
- tables can be placed in front of the seats, they can be easy chairs, or 'student-type' chairs with a flat arm to take a notepad
- the trainer has good visibility of all the learners and can therefore maintain good eye contact, and is not behind a table/desk barrier although one is near at hand for briefs, handouts and as a video table when necessary
- the seating configuration can be easily altered, for example for buzz groups or paired discussions
- The OHP is readily available
- The video can be kept in readiness, but out of the way, to be placed on the trainer's table when required
- The screen is easily visible from most of the learner positions
- The tables at the back of the room can be used for reference material, computer positions or as refreshment tables if these are to be taken in the training room.

9   The Use of Training Aids

▷   CHAPTER SUMMARY   ◁

This chapter:

- extends the skills and activities necessary to present an effective training session
- describes the use of visual aids in training, in particular the flipchart, the whiteboard and the overhead projector.

Visual Aids

One of the more important skills for a trainer, a skill that will help them to improve and add variety to their presentations, is the effective use of training aids. The new trainer will be unlikely to have recourse to or need to use the full range of aids, certainly in their earlier stages, so during this programme concentration on the simpler visual aids will be most appropriate. The wider range and the advanced use of aids can be left for a later module.

This stage of the TDP can concentrate on five aids, three of which are equipment-based – the flipchart, the whiteboard and the overhead projector (OHP). Most new trainers will find they can/are expected to use one or all of these, although in some older establishments the traditional chalkboard (blackboard – even though it may be green) is still the major piece of equipment. The type of training will also have an influence on any aids used or not used. One-to-one desk training on, for example, computer applications will require none of these, the principal aids being the computer hardware and software themselves. Most training, however, benefits from the use of some form of aid, the more realistic the better.

Variation of Session Approach

A training session on this subject can be presented in a variety of ways, depending on the prior knowledge of the learners – many will have attended previous training courses as learners so will at least have seen some of the aids in use by the trainers; others may have a restricted knowledge or experience (recently I met a trainer with seven years experience who, during that time had not used an OHP and knew very little about them; she had had no reason to use one in the type of training she had performed to that point). Yet others may have no knowledge whatsoever about training aids.

In the case of a group of learners in the last category, it will be necessary to run full sessions starting with a physical description and demonstration of the equipment and the ways it can be used. For those with restricted knowledge, either of the range of aids or the more advanced uses of them, the session can concentrate on either the unknown aids or input, with demonstration and practice in the more advanced techniques. The session for those with some knowledge but little or no skill will be a mixture of the two, the depth of content depending on the level of knowledge and skill.

Here I will discuss the middle range approach – learners who have some, albeit limited, knowledge and skill in the subject.

The Visual Aid Learning Session

The five most commonly used training aids are machines, system manuals, equipment, etc; the trainers themselves; the overhead projector and its accompanying slides; the flipchart and the whiteboard.

The session can concentrate on these training aids and give the learners the opportunity to practise and experiment with them. In order to ensure that the learners with little or no knowledge of training aids and those with a limited knowledge, a brief input should precede the practical activities.

Training in the use of a training aid is most effective when the aid itself is to hand. In some cases this will not be possible and the trainer may need to use a photograph of the object, passed round the learners or projected; an OHP diagram; a computer graphic; an audio recording (for an audio object); or a video recording, particularly where a sequence is involved (even home camcorders can be valuable for this purpose).

DESIGN APPLICATION 23

The object as a visual aid requires little verbal description – objects speak for themselves and so make effective training aids. The trainer can demonstrate this use, for example with an OHP, using the 'Tell, Show, Do' technique. The OHP can be described verbally as an instrument used to support the trainer during an input session; the OHP itself can then be revealed and described in detail. Finally, the learners can be given the opportunity to handle the OHP.

This approach can be used for many objects, although some will require careful handling both by the trainer and the learners.

The Trainer as a Visual Aid

Although many trainers may not appreciate the fact, they are themselves one of the most powerful and visible visual aids, aids which can have a considerable impact on the learners. This is particularly so in the case of trainer training. The learners are seeking knowledge, advice, guidance and skills in an area in which they will soon be practising. The trainer is helping them along this path and the learners naturally assume (hopefully correctly) that their mentor is a skilled, experienced and effective trainer. Consequently there will be some role modelling – consciously or subconsciously. This is not to be encouraged as the learners should develop their own styles, but mimicry is natural, particularly if the trainer is especially effective (and popular).

In an attempt to try to avoid this role modelling, the introduction of a number of trainers into the programme, particularly if they have different styles, can be valuable. It can, of course, have the reverse effect of helping the learners to compare (sometimes unfavourably rather than as different styles) training and trainer styles.

Flipcharts, Whiteboards and Overhead Projectors

The simplest, but not necessarily the most appropriate nor effective, approach to the subject is to present a full input session, describing the equipment, the advantages and disadvantages, the methods of use and advanced techniques. This could be a very substantial input and, although it may be appropriate in some situations, generally there are more effective ways.

One approach that I have found to be effective, particularly with a learning group which contains a mixture of knowledge and skill levels, would take the pattern shown in design application 24.

DESIGN APPLICATION 24

- Give a brief description of the basic features of each of the three training aids
- Divide the learning group into three sub-groups selected for the most appropriate mix of those with full, some and no knowledge and skills
- Allocate one of the three aids to each group
- Ask the learners to discuss their allocated aid and pool their knowledge
- Ask the learners to identify and list the advantages and disadvantages of the aid
- Each sub-group will present their findings to the other groups, treating the report-back as a semi-formal presentation, utilizing various techniques and certainly involving the aid itself.

The principal role of the trainer in this event is to organize the groups, make equipment available, be available as a resource to the learners and, after the presentations, to pick up significant learning points not made. For example, the OHP group might omit comments on turning to the screen to point out entries: the trainer would add this in a brief, but impactive comment.

Some of the areas that the trainer should have noted in preparation for the report-back session will include the following:

Flipcharts

Advantages

- *Transportable* – the flipchart can be easily rolled up and the easel can be collapsed for carrying
- *No Power* – unlike the OHP, slide projector, video, etc, no power supply is required so it is not susceptible to power failures or the lack of suitably positioned power points
- *Adaptable* – can be used as a blank sheet on which items can be added or as a prepared sheet, the contents of which can be disclosed in a variety of ways
- *Any paper usable* – the 'flipchart paper' itself need not be a commercial flipchart; any large sheet of paper can be used
- *Easy to use* – few basic skills, other than those of clear writing, are required
- *Retained for reference* – each sheet used can be torn from the flipchart pad and retained as a poster on the training room wall
- *Simple, cheap, needs little training* – a principal advantage: the training necessary perhaps including skills in large, clear writing and using various techniques for impact and use

- *Usable for immediate recording* – no pre-preparation is necessary if it is to be used as a large jotting pad during a training session
- *Postable anywhere* – sheets of paper, even the A1 size of the normal flipchart, are relatively light and can be posted on walls, doors, cabinets, and even curtains, using a dry, re-usable adhesive such as BluTack.

Disadvantages

- *If badly prepared, can look unprofessional* – a poor appearance can be off-putting to the learners and the trainer's credibility can be reduced
- *Usually of only a temporary value* – because paper is used, this medium will have a limited life which can reduce the value of the aid if it is important enough to be retained and re-used
- *Easily torn, dirtied and dog-eared* – although easily portable, it is also easy to damage the sheets in transit or in storage
- *Special techniques difficult* – there are some special techniques relevant to the use of flipcharts and these can take a certain amount of skill and dexterity. For example, a disclosure approach using covering cards held by BluTack or paper clips can be used, or constant reference back and forward to various sheets can be helped with folds and clips - both these techniques can go wrong so easily.

The whiteboard

The whiteboard, which is the modern equivalent of the chalkboard, has many similarities with the flipchart. It is less portable, usually being much larger (although whiteboards as small as 6 inches by 4 inches can be obtained); it can be easel- or wall-mounted. Entries can be erased – which is both an advantage and a disadvantage: the board can be continuously used and re-used, but unless you have more than one board, entered material cannot be retained. Some advanced whiteboards have more than one 'board' which can be displayed electrically and others have a photocopying facility so that the entered data can be copied onto A4 paper – a useful means of producing an immediate handout.

The overhead projector

Advantages

- *High visual impact* – because the image is projected by a light source, the visual impact can be high compared with a rather dull flipchart
- *Usable in light* – unlike slide and film projectors, the room does not

need to be darkened and so the trainer has continuous eye contact with the learning group

- *Large image* – the projected image can be large, the actual size limited only by the size of the screen or projections area, the light intensity of the projector and the type of lens used
- *OHPs widely available* – this item of equipment is nowadays almost as freely available in many locations as the flipchart; if it is not available where required, it is easily transportable, particularly portable models
- *Used sitting or standing* – some trainers prefer to sit while presenting, others prefer to stand and/or walk about; the OHP permits either method of use, although it was designed for the trainer to be seated beside it
- *Professional production* – OHP slides can have a very professional appearance, whether they are made skilfully by hand, by commercial photographic techniques, or, more commonly now, as a computer graphic
- *Slides easily portable* – the acetate slides used with the OHP can be carried easily in a folder, briefcase or slide carrying case.

Disadvantages

Power required – unlike, for example the flipchart, an electric power source is required. Under most conditions this will not be a problem, but power failures still occur when the OHP cannot be operated, or suitable power sockets are not available and the trainer does not have a converter plug

Noise – older (and modern but cheaper) OHP models are cooled by a fan which can be very noisy in operation

Condition variable – many OHPs are older, well-used models which can be in a poor condition

Head post can obscure – part of an OHP is the angled mirror mounted at the top of a column; this head can obscure part of the screen image from some of the group unless particular care is taken in seating arrangements

Keystoning – the off-putting effect of keystoning – when the top of the projected image is wider horizontally than the base, usually the result of a too acute angle of projection; it can sometimes be difficult to rectify

Crowded slide encouragement – an acetate sheet from which OHP slides are produced can tempt the trainer to include too much material on one slide. A major advantage of the OHP is its possibility for impact – overcrowding reduces this possibility.

Flipcharts, Whiteboards and Overhead Projectors – Common Factors

Certain aspects of the use of these aids are common to all three. The trainer can introduce this area in a brief input – brief to avoid over-passivity by the learning group, and because they can later be asked to look more closely at these and other areas and present their own findings (see design application 25). The aspects can be considered under the headings:

- *Legibility* – each aid has specific requirements for size regarding entries, based on the distance from the aid of the furthest learner, the lighting conditions and so on.
- *Writing on the medium* – writing or drawing on all the aids is different from making the same entries on, for example, an A4 sheet of paper. Trainers must practise these different skills to ensure a professional approach which links with the legibility issue. There are also physical requirements concerned with writing – keeping lines horizontal, not talking to the flipchart, and not writing on the projection screen (it does happen!).
- *Use of colour, etc* – there are many opportunities in the use of visual aids to add impact to the message. This can be achieved by such means as a use of colour, underlining, upper and lower case, boxing entries and so on.
- *Methods and Materials used* – all the aids being considered can be used in a variety of ways with a range of methods and materials – writing, drawings, graphs, cards to hide or disclose – varying these can add further impact.

DESIGN APPLICATION 25

1. Put the learning group back into their three sub-groups
2. Ask them to consider all aspects of the aids selected – descriptions of the aids, advantages and disadvantages, common features and uses
3. Each sub-group should prepare a presentation on its selected aid, using the aid and involving all the members of the group in the presentation to the trainer and the other groups.

Following the presentations by the sub-groups and discussion on the presentations, supplemented as necessary by the trainer, the session can be rounded-off by the trainer offering a number of 'golden rules' in the use of these aids. These will include:

Flipchart

- It should be clear enough and the writing large enough to be read from anywhere in the training room
- When its use is complete, flip over to a blank sheet
- Do not write and talk while facing the flipchart. If you must write and talk at the same time, stand to one side of the flipchart. But it is better to stop talking, write, then recommence talking.

Whiteboard

- All the flipchart rules apply, but remember to use the correct dry marker pen
- Remember that it is only too easy for whiteboard entries to be erased.

Overhead projector

- Point to the slide on the projector not to the screen
- Switch off as soon as you have finished with a slide, but on/off, on/off, on/off in swift succession is even worse than leaving it on.

The Construction of Visual Aids

The new trainer must learn to produce visual aids themselves in addition to using the equipment effectively. Some mention has been made earlier about some of the common aspects of the three aids under discussion – legibility, impact, the use of colour and so on. These aspects can and should be included in the normal use of the visual aids. However, there are some special techniques that can be used to improve the effectiveness and the impact of the aids. Some of these are applicable to the flipchart, some to the whiteboard, some to the OHP and some to all.

The trainer can describe and demonstrate the variations possible in these media. These can include:

- disclosure techniques – all the three media
- additive techniques – all the three media
- pencil guide lines for lines or words – flipchart.

Even the most charismatic speaker's event can be improved by the judicious and effective use of training aids. Care must be taken not to overdo these supports as learners can become as tired of too many visual aids as of too much talking. But they can enhance a presentation both by making it more interesting and also ensuring that the verbal message is sufficiently supported to be understood and remembered more easily than from the spoken word alone.

10 In Front of the Group

▷   **CHAPTER SUMMARY**   ◁

This chapter:

- extends the skills and activities necessary to present an effective training session
- describes the structure of a training session or presentation for maximum effectiveness
- details techniques for controlling the effects of stress on presenters
- describes verbal and non-verbal pitfalls and gives advice on methods to avoid these.

Introduction

Early in the career of a new trainer, hopefully with the preparation completed and visual aids prepared as described in the preceding chapters, the time will come for the trainer to face a group of learners to present a training session of the input variety. In order to succeed, the trainer must possess at least the basic presentational skills – not everybody is a natural, charismatic speaker; most have to work hard to achieve some form of acceptance.

For someone new to facing an audience or training group, the event is a traumatic one which is rated in most surveys as being a greater cause of concern or fear even than death and other serious incidents.

The presenter will have prepared the session material and will have a session brief of the type which has been found to be the most personally useful. Visual aids will have been prepared where necessary or the trainer will be prepared and able to produce them during the session. All pre-session checks will have been made and the trainer is now ready to face the group, or as many trainers put it, 'take the stage'. This expression is very relevant because the trainer in front of a group, although not an actor, is a 'performer' in the widest sense of the word.

The format of the session will have either been determined for the trainer by the organization, training manager or senior trainer, or some latitude will have been given for the new trainer to personalize the session to some extent.

The Normal Effect

Because presenting to a group causes stress for most people – and many never overcome this – the new trainer will be suffering a number of effects. The more normal symptom is 'butterflies' in the stomach and in some extreme cases nausea and even actual sickness. The trainer must ensure that the learners are aware that this is a very common effect, experienced by almost every trainer, presenter, actor and anyone who has to appear in public as the centre of attention with some action to perform. Many well-known 'stars' admit to physical sickness before going on stage for the first appearance. Usually, once the ice has been broken, the butterflies should disappear or reduce considerably.

Although the new trainers might not be in a state of mind to accept what you say, it is often useful to let the learners know what sort of feelings you have when you start a course or session. At least they will realize that you can relate personally to their own feelings.

Preventing Presentation Stress

It must be accepted that the stress at the start of a presentation or training session can never be completely removed – it may not in fact be desirable unless the symptoms become too strong and interfere with the presentation. A certain amount of stress lets us know that we are concerned about our effectiveness and the extent to which we shall be helping the learners. The ones who have no nerves or nervousness at all, even covert feelings, are usually those who do not care whether they are successful or not, nor whether or not the learners achieve something from their intervention.

Attempts at prevention or at least alleviation of the symptoms are those usually connected with stress release. Many people find relief through deliberate, slow, deep breathing; others by thinking clearly about what they are going to do; others by some form of yoga exercise. But rarely do the butterfly nerves completely disappear until the presentation is under way.

Initial Action

The first intention of the trainer must be to try to avoid letting the audience/group of learners see the extent of the nervousness. Even though they themselves may have been in the same position, have experienced the same feelings and have sympathy for the presenter, there will still be suspicion of ability about someone who exhibits major nervousness.

When we are nervous the throat dries up, the heart starts beating swiftly and we start talking much more quickly. So:

- have a drink of water to help lubricate the throat (not too much)
- breathe deeply and slowly to help slow down the heart rate
- when you start talking, do so much more slowly than you would normally – you may even then think you are talking too slowly, but this is most unlikely
- be over-deliberate in your speech and over-enunciate – you may think it will be very obvious; not so, because all you will be doing will be compensating for the effects of nerves
- as soon as possible involve the group by asking a question or asking their views on something – this brings them in and allows you some time to settle down now that you are on stage
- be absolutely sure of what you are going to say at the start, even to the extent of having memorized the words. The most difficult part of the presentation is getting going, so if you are confident about that, the remainder of the session should have few problems of this nature.

The Basic Format of the Session or Presentation

Whatever the nature of the session in which the trainer is going to be involved, unless it is entirely an information-seeking situation, you are going to be involved in telling the audience something, usually by a variety of means. So start the event by a 'telling openness':

- Tell them what you're going to tell them – the introduction.

The initial 'tell them' is a short statement of the main items to be included in the session, the objectives, and any special aspects of this content.

After this introduction you will be in the main body of the session, so:

- Tell them – the main section of your message.

When you have delivered the material you set out to present:

- Tell them what you've told them – a summary of the presentation.

The Opening

There is rarely a second chance to make a first impression! So if you can start confidently as suggested, the next thing is to start with a bang, not a whimper. A 'bang' can be:

- a dramatic statement
- a provocative or controversial statement or question
- a *relevant* humorous anecdote or story – not a joke
- an impactive visual aid, a brief item on an audio tape or video
- a model or example of the subject, perhaps presented theatrically
- an unexpected entry to the training room or a gimmicky introduction.

Vocal Presentation

Knowing what you are going to say during your session is a major ingredient in the recipe for success, but during a learning event, the trainer's voice is also an important aspect of the presentation.

DESIGN APPLICATION 26

- As an alternative to purely telling the learners what to do with their voices, it can be useful to put them into sub-groups with the brief to identify and list as many characteristics of an effective speaker as they can, drawing on their own experiences as listeners. They can consider good and bad speakers they have known and analyse why they have given them these labels.
- An alternative can be to ask the learners, as individuals, to list the characteristics of a bad speaker or speakers they have encountered.
- In both cases the subsequent action is a discussion to identify the factors that go towards producing a 'good' speaker.

A number of characteristics will emerge as a result of the discussions suggested above; these will include:

- accent difficult to understand
- boring, monotonous voice
- didn't look at the group once
- lack of projection
- material not presented in a logical manner
- over-hesitant
- over-repetitive
- played with a pen all the time
- played with money and keys in pocket the whole time
- prowled about all the time
- too many 'er', 'hmm', 'ums'
- uninterested and disinterested manner
- uninteresting material
- used too much jargon or complicated words which couldn't be understood
- wasn't enthusiastic about the subject

and so on.

The lists will vary from group to group, but as in the list above, both verbal and non-verbal characteristics will emerge. Reference can be made to the discussion on communication which will have been held earlier in the programme (see Chapter 6).

Using the Voice for Impact

The principal tool of a trainer is the voice. Some voices are effective, others rarely make an impact, with a full range in between these extremes. Trainers must be aware of their voice and the effect it is having on their listeners – a good message fails if nobody listens to it.

Fortunately we are in a position to take control of our voice to give more impact. Although we have what might be termed an ordinary voice that we use under 'normal' situations, this voice has remarkable variation qualities. We can deliberately modify our voice in many ways and this will certainly be required during training presentations if the session is to have any interest for the learners.

Parents will recognize this immediately if they recall how they sounded when telling their teenager to get off the phone, compared with when they were asking their boss for a favour, when they were at the football match and their local team was winning/losing, and so on. This means that if a different vocal ploy is needed, such a change is relatively easy to achieve.

DESIGN APPLICATION 27

To demonstrate how the voice can be varied, and its significance:

- select seven learners from the group
- ask each to repeat the phrase 'I asked you yesterday, leave me alone'
- each should emphasize in turn one word in the phrase.

The change implications should be discussed after the demonstration.

There are two simple mnemonics that can help you remember how to control your voice effectively.

The 4 Ps:

Project your voice by altering the volume

Pronounce your words carefully, control as far as possible any strong accent, and check beforehand the pronunciation or correct use of any words about which you are uncertain

Pause. Frequent pauses break a train of words, vary the flow, make it more interesting and allow the listeners to catch up

Pace. Vary the pace and the presentation will be varied. Speed up to excite, enthuse, suggest importance; slow down to emphasize, to explain a complexity, to make a dramatic effect.

MERK:

Modulate the tone of your voice to keep it interesting – use drama, apparent monotony, harshness, softness and so on

Emphasize certain parts of the speech for effect

Repeat key words and phrases to emphasize their importance and ensure understanding and recall

Keep you eyes away from your notes, otherwise your volume will drop, you may seem to mumble and your credibility will reduce if it appears that you are just reading from a script.

Physical Platform Presence

There are many other factors which can affect the degree of impact you are making in your presentation. These include a number of physical factors – how you look, what you do and the mannerisms you have.

Appearance

There can be no set rules for how a trainer should dress – much will depend on the sex of the trainer, their personal dress preferences, the culture of the organization, etc. The principal guideline, however, must be that the appearance of the trainer must not interfere with the learning. If, for example, the learning group appear smartly dressed and turned out and the trainer is untidy and differently attired, the learners *may* for a while fail to learn because they are too interested in the trainer's differences to take any notice of what he or she is saying.

Mannerisms

These fall under the general heading of non-verbal communication and behaviour. There is nothing wrong with a mannerism as long as it does not become a barrier to communication between you and the learners. Some common mannerisms exhibited by trainers/presenters in front of a group are discussed below:

Movement If you are the type of person who cannot sit and must move about, do so. Not to do so would make you feel uneasy and unnatural, which would have an adverse effect on your presentation with a reduction in the learning. But avoid pacing about like a caged lion – the learners will stop listening to you and watch you pacing.

Many people are unable to talk without also moving their arms about. Again, if this is part of your normal and natural behaviour, do not restrain it, although you must ensure that it does not become too intrusive.

Movement can add to your presentation. When you reach a particularly important part, if you have been sitting, stand up to deliver the relevant part, then sit down again. This must not be repeated too often otherwise you may appear like a yo-yo!

Vocal mannerisms There are many variations in this area. For example, if you are nervous, your 'er' rate will increase considerably, particularly at the start of a sentence when you have paused prior to this. 'Er, the widget that goes into the, er, sprog hole will not fit easily if, er, the sides are rough. Er, so you must ensure, er...'. If you notice, perhaps accidentally, that you are doing this during your talking, there is a danger that you may even increase the number of incidences. However, if you do notice or have it pointed out to you, concentrate when you reach the danger spots in your material – areas of which you are unsure, pauses and so on – and try not to 'er'. You will not always be successful in this, but you will avoid the learning group logging the number of times you say 'er'.

Listen to yourself critically on a videoed presentation, practice or real-time, preferably with a colleague, and try to identify any other vocal mannerisms you exhibit, *the frequency of which can interfere with a learning situation.*

One of the overt signs of nervousness is when the trainer or presenter, instead of presenting material in a logical, clear manner, babbles on with continuous repetitions and irrelevant statements. To avoid this keep the KISS principle firmly in mind – Keep It Short and Simple. Ask yourself as you present 'What am I doing? Kissing or babbling?'.

Physical mannerisms Are you a pen or pencil player? Even worse, while you are talking do you in addition to playing with an OHP or flipchart pen, juggle with it? If so, stop! In general avoid playing with the props – you may upset something and if the frequency reaches a certain level, the learners will be watching you and anticipating what might happen next.

Nowadays there are general injunctions against smoking in a training room. This should certainly apply to the trainer as taking a cigarette from the packet, trying to light it while talking, putting the cigarette in your mouth just as somebody asks a question – these are all pitfalls to avoid. The avoidance is simple: don't smoke.

One of the disturbing mannerisms exhibited by men is constantly jingling keys and money in their trouser pockets – keep your hands out of your pockets. Women exhibit similarly nervousness-based mannerisms by fiddling with their hair, often twisting longer parts round their fingers.

I attended a presentation session during which the speaker gazed over the heads of the group, at the clock at the rear of the room. We felt that he wasn't sufficiently interested in us as a group to look at us and that he was more interested in his finishing time than the period preceding it. This of course was not so, but wrong signals were being sent, signals that were certainly read as they were sent by some members of the group.

If you are talking to a group of people, remember they are people and look at them as you talk – *all of them.* It is only too easy to identify an apparently friendly looking face and concentrate on talking to that person to the exclusion of others. As you talk, look around all the group, ensuring that you look at all parts of the group. But do not be a search-light, regularly sweeping your gaze round and round. Make the movements natural, but beware the extremities! If the group is sitting in the typical U-shape, the learners at the ends of the U are more likely to be ignored, so it may need a deliberate action to look at these people.

You will find a myriad of books to help you in the design of sessions concerned with presenting yourself and material, verbal and non-verbal activities, behavioural attitudes and so on. There has been considerable research into this subject which is obviously reflected in the amount of published literature. You and the learners will benefit from reading this literature and selecting tips and techniques, but the maximum benefit in developing presentation skills will always be in practice and real presentations, preferably with effective feedback. This should be borne in mind when you are allocating programme time between input sessions on presenting and practice/feedback sessions.

11 Completing the Programme (1)

┌───┐
▷   CHAPTER SUMMARY   ◁

This chapter:

- suggests other sessions that can be usefully included in a TDP
- describes the basic aspects of these sessions
- suggests material and design applications that can be included
- considers:
  – activities in training
  – aims and objectives
  – CCTV and its place in training
  – discussion-leading skills

The remaining sessions are described in Chapter 12.
└───┘

In addition to the material contained in the preceding chapter, other topics should be contained if at all possible within the two-week structure. These continue the theme of providing only what the majority of new trainers require in the early stages of their careers. Space does not permit full descriptions of this material – the source books will provide these – so summaries of the content and approaches are given. The sessions recommended for inclusion are those concerned with:

- Activities in training
- Aims and objectives
- CCTV and its place in training
- Discussion-leading skills
- Listening skills

- Observation and feedback skills
- Questioning skills
- Role plays
- Videos and their effective use.

Activities in Training

Although not every training programme provides the opportunity to include activities, this session is included in the TDP to guide learners in the use of activities and to encourage them to look beyond the traditional input form of training. Practical activities, exercises, icebreakers and games satisfy the 'doing' sector of the learning cycle – part of the essential whole. They may at times seem too informal, even childish to some of the learners, but they must be planned, introduced and implemented so that the learners have the opportunity to extract the deliberate learning points either during the activity or the essential review/feedback session following the activity.

The training and development literature includes a large number and variety of publications which give full information on activities for virtually every situation. In fact there is an embarrassment of these publications and the problem has now become one of literature search to find the most appropriate activity. (See 'Activities for Trainers – A Bane or a Boon', Leslie Rae, *Training Officer*, Vol 29, No 10, December 1993).

A situation that the trainer should avoid is to include so many activities that the learning event becomes known as the 'game course'. The criterion for any form of training is to use the most appropriate mixture of approaches to the most appropriate extent without overloading the event with any one approach.

Consideration should also be given to the use of observers taken from the learning group. It is frequently said that the observer sees/learns more than the participant – this may be true, but the observers must know what they are looking for if they are to learn themselves and provide feedback information of value to the participants. This may involve a session during the event on observation (feedback will be covered elsewhere) or the trainer can give the observers a mini teach-in while the participants are reading the activity brief and preparing for it. The major problem with unskilled observers is that, if there are several, they may all view an incident in different ways and give conflicting feedback.

The approach to this session should follow the basic premise of the subject – namely the use of activities – so input should be at a minimum. Two particular aspects of activities can be brought out at the start of the session following a brief introduction about the nature of activities. These activities are described in the design applications 28 and 29.

DESIGN APPLICATION 28

- Divide the learning group into two sub-groups, one to identify, discuss and list on the flipchart for presentation to the other group the reasons for using, and the benefits of, activities. The other group should perform a similar activity but looking at the disadvantages of activities.
- Both groups should then report back in full group with discussion.

The lists should include the following:

Can be used –
- as icebreakers
- as energizers
- as motivators
- to reinforce learning points
- to replace an input to produce learning points
- to change the pace
- to introduce activity from passivity
- for team building
- to validate learning
- to encourage group responsibility
- to introduce most or all parts of the learning cycle
- for quick impact as a short activity
- to mix groups and individuals
- to get everybody involved.

Disadvantages –
- can be risky to trainer and learners
- can be seen as playing games
- can be thought irrelevant
- can create 'winners' and 'losers'
- individuals might feel exposed
- may be difficult to time
- may need expensive equipment
- may need lots of space
- may need lots of time
- needs effective control
- needs lots of organizing
- not real life.

Points to Watch when Running Activities

Some of the problems outlined above can be avoided using these guidelines:

Setting up	Running	Reviewing
Understand aims of the exercise	Monitor progress	Immediate reactions
Check all materials and equipment	Observe who is doing what, where and when	Give support and feedback
Check timings	Check on timings	Discuss task
Ensure basic brief is understood	Control if necessary	Discuss process
Brief fully	Never interrupt, unless getting dangerous	Relate back to work
Have some idea of likely outcome/ lessons to be learned		Look at lessons learned
Check understanding		Do not belittle efforts

Whatever method or approach, or mixture of approaches is used by the trainer, it must be fully understood *why* that method is being used, *how* it can be used most effectively, and that it is the most appropriate approach for that situation. The trainer must consider these questions during the design stage and review them during the implementation of the event – different and changing situations often call for a modification of the existing design. The trainer should have a 'toolkit' of methods with which he or she is very familiar which can be introduced at the relevant and appropriate times. A major danger to avoid is to become locked-in to a particular activity, set of activities or methods to the exclusion of all others, even when the preferred approach is obviously not the most appropriate.

DESIGN APPLICATION 29

The input material should be followed by a practical activity which should be run as far as possible by the learners, divided into three groups – the 'trainer' group who should be responsible for running the activity and controlling the review; the 'player' group who take part in the activity; and the 'observer' group who observe and report on the manner in which the players carry out the activity and how the trainers set up and brief for the activity and run the review.

Aims and Objectives

DESIGN APPLICATION 30

The benefits of producing and using aims and objectives can be brought out from the learner group in either a full group discussion or in sub-group 'buzz' groups.

The types of comments you can expect to emerge and which you will be seeking will include:

- Writer and trainer will have clear goals
- Will help structuring of the material
- Need to be correctly set, are realistic and achievable in time allowed
- When quoted, the learners know what is expected of them
- Learners know what is expected of them by the end of the session
- Gives the learners signposts to help them through the session
- Enables validation of the training material and techniques.

Methods

The obvious method of making the objectives known to the learners is for the trainer to state them at the start of the session; this may not be the most appropriate method on every occasion and other methods include:

- Verbally by the trainer at start of session – least useful as the comments can be easily forgotten by both trainer and learner
- In advance of course with the course programme
- On an OHP slide – projected at the start of the session while the trainer explains them
- On a handout – as handouts are usually most effectively issued at the end of the session, this will be one of the least successful

- On a flipchart sheet – probably the most effective. If the trainer posts this flipchart at the start of the session with any necessary explanations, it can be left posted for reference at any time during the session and at the end, when achievement of the objectives is being considered.

Activities

Activities are a valuable way to give the learners practice in the use of aims and objectives and to demonstrate how they can be used with effect. Two activities can be recommended and are given in design applications 31 and 32.

DESIGN APPLICATION 31

Divide the learning group into two sub-groups. Issue an example of a poorly written objective and ask the sub-groups to:

- identify why it is an ineffective objective statement
- rewrite the objective to make it effective
- ask each group to present its findings to the trainer and the other group and discuss the views.

DESIGN APPLICATION 32

- Divide the learning group into pairs and ask them to write the aims and objectives for a training session they are going to write and present on a hobby, interest or pastime. The subject will be decided within the pairs.
- Ask each pair to produce a flipchart showing the title of their session, the aim(s) and the objectives. The session should then be written in basic summary format, ie the steps that will be followed during the session.
- Reconvene the group and ask each pair to present briefly what they have produced, the emphasis being on the objectives – other pairs can be invited to comment.

Summary

An essential element of the presentation techniques of the TDP is that they should put into practice what they preach and this practice should be observable by the learners. This is especially important in the case of aims and objectives.

DESIGN APPLICATION 33

Review the session by returning to the stated objectives for the session. Show the group how this can be useful to summarize a session and bring it to an effective conclusion.

CCTV and its Place in Training

A session of this nature will be a very practical one, with the minimum input by the trainer being a demonstration of the video camera and its associated equipment. Many learners will already have some familiarity with video equipment, with the widespread use of home camcorders. The point will obviously have to be made that equipment might vary from location to location, but the basics are all very similar.

Following the demonstration and description, ample opportunity must be given for the learners to have 'hands-on' experience, initially just 'playing' with the equipment under the supervision of the trainer. They can then be arranged in groups – the size dependent on how many sets of equipment are available – to record some activity. One group could be performing an activity while a pair, for example, might be recording the event, having set up the location and the equipment. Groups can take turns in these roles.

Advantages and Disadvantages

When the group has had sufficient familiarization time with the equipment, a discussion can be held on the uses of CCTV and in particular its advantages and disadvantages.

DESIGN APPLICATION 34

- Divide the learning group into two sub-groups.
- Group 1 should discuss and list the advantages of using CCTV in training.
- Group 2 should discuss and list the problems that can arise in using CCTV.

Following the activity, the sub-groups should present their findings to the other group and the trainers and the results should be discussed with a view to obtaining clarity and completeness.

A trainer-led discussion can follow these presentations, concentrating on how the advantages might be utilized and the barriers minimized. The advantages discussed should include:

- fully objective and honest observation
- instant feedback on skills, personal styles, mannerisms
- captures audience reaction to events
- accurate and complete recall
- feedback can be isolated into significant incidents
- observation can be remote – observers in another room
- small groups can work on their own.

The barriers would include:

- feedback using CCTV recordings can take a lot more time
- an effective introduction is necessary about why CCTV is being used
- people may be sensitive about being filmed
- the equipment can be obtrusive
- those filmed tend to concentrate on mannerisms when viewing, rather than functions
- somebody is needed to set it up and operate it
- used less effectively if camera operator is the sole trainer
- some equipment is cumbersome and complex.

Discussion-leading Skills

In the learner-centred, maximum participation TDP that I am recommending, trainers will be involved in discussion with their learning groups to a much greater extent than when they give traditional-style presentation sessions. Many new trainers believe that discussion is 'simply' having the learners talk about some subject, and that they will do this easily. This feeling relates to both ad hoc discussions during a session and also specific discussion sessions arranged as such.

Nothing could be further from the truth as any experienced trainer knows – if handled badly, attempts to induce discussion during a session can result in total failure. A discussion session scheduled for, say 30 minutes, can be 'complete' at the end of five.

Introducing the Subject

Before the session enters a more practical stage, two identification activities can be held, using either buzz groups or sub-groups which will report back their findings, or a full group discussion to have the information emerge.

Reasons for using discussion

DESIGN APPLICATION 35

- Ask the learning group what they consider would be the reasons for introducing discussion into a training event.
- Record the responses on flipchart.

The reasons that emerge should include:

- problem-solving sessions
- decision-making sessions
- changing attitudes
- encouraging attitudes, views and opinions to emerge
- development of leadership skills
- involvement of all group members
- a supplementary training technique
- an interruption of the trainer's 'monologue'
- encourages all members to talk.

DESIGN APPLICATION 36

- Divide the learning group into two sub-groups and ask them both to identify the advantages of discussion over other training techniques and also its disadvantages.
- These should be listed on flipchart for presentation to the trainer and the other group after the activity.

The advantages and disadvantages that emerge should include:

Advantages
- adds variety to an input training session
- all learners are involved in an effective discussion

- the views of the learners emerge, not just those of the trainer
- a subject theme can be developed without a long input session
- participants are stimulated to contribute and be interested
- the discussion helps learners to crystallize their thoughts, views and opinions
- demonstrates to the learners the views of others in the group
- demonstrates to the learners that there are views other than their own
- the skill and experience of the learners are utilized.

Disadvantages
- can be a time-consuming activity
- unless led effectively, can degenerate into a purposeless conversation or an argument between members.

Practical 'Discussion' Demonstration

DESIGN APPLICATION 37

- The subject of discussion-leading skills can be introduced successfully by a demonstration discussion group, led by the trainer who will perform as many errors and discussion-leading faults as possible – overtalking the members, constantly giving his or her own opinions, ignoring quiet members, allowing sidetalking and so on.
- After the necessary period of time – usually about 10 minutes – the participants and the rest of the learners who have been observing can identify and list the errors and decide the effective and desirable techniques compared with the demonstrated ineffective ones.

Although not requiring preparation to the same extent as for a presentation, there must be some careful preparation by the trainer if the discussion is to be successful. There is little need for the trainer to pretend that he or she is 'hamming' it – this is usually obvious at least to the observing members, although often the participants become so involved and sometimes either overtly or covertly emotional that they do not realize what is happening. It can also be useful to have at least one 'plant' who might be the constant side-talker or interrupter who gets away with it.

Structure and Methods

Design application 37 should enable a lot of views about discussions and discussion-leading to emerge; the trainer can follow this by concentrating input and discussion on two specific aspects of the subject, briefs and the discussion itself.

Discussion-leading Briefs

Although the 'brief' for a discussion will not be as extensive or complex as that prepared for a presentation, a form of brief is necessary, even if just to remind the discussion leader what has to be covered – this can refer to either a full discussion session or, in a rather more limited way, to the lesser discussions planned to take place during a session.

Two principal types of brief are in common use, the choice usually depending on the type of discussion to take place.

The shopping list

This type of reminder simply lists the various parts of the discussion subject that should or might be covered. As the discussion progresses, the items covered can be struck through or ticked off. When discussion falters, subject parts not yet covered can be easily identified and introduced.

Pro and con list

Where there is likely to be a considerable amount of controversy about a subject, with different members taking opposing views, a pro and con list can be produced prior to the discussion, including as many of the summarized arguments as the leader can identify.

Divide an A4 sheet of paper vertically, the left side being headed 'Pro' and the right side 'Con'. List the various aspects on each side. During the discussion, as with the shopping list, annotate the subjects covered and use the remainder as reminders of parts of the subject or argument areas not yet introduced.

Preparation

As in the case of every form of training and development, preparation is the key to success. The following guidelines can either be presented by the trainer or developed from an activity using sub-groups of learners to produce their views:

- Determine your objectives for initiating discussion; these usually fall into one of four principal areas:

- to reinforce learning points recently presented
- to exchange views, information and feelings
- to encourage the learners to talk
- as a break in a trainer presentation and to change passivity to activity.

- Select a topic which will lead to satisfaction of your objectives – this will obviously depend on the situation. In a TDP, if a practice discussion is included, the choice of subject may not necessarily be important.

- Devise a suitable opening for the discussion. Frequently, the most difficult part of a discussion is ensuring that, having introduced it, discussion actually starts. The trainer has a very positive role to play at this stage. In a similar way to a presentation opening, starting with a form of 'bang' can help to start the discussion:
  - make a controversial statement and invite discussion
  - use a gimmick to involve the learners
  - play part of a video or audio recording
  - refer to a role play, simulation or case study
  - refer to a newspaper headline.

- Prepare your discussion 'brief' – either as a shopping list or a table of pros and cons, depending on the nature of the subject.

- Make the physical and environmental arrangements.

Running the Session

The golden rule for the trainer or discussion leader must be that, having opened the discussion, they take as little part as possible in the actual discussion. The role of the discussion leader is to ensure that the environment is conducive to encouraging the group members to hold the discussion and contribute. The discussion leader's role is one of monitor, controller and facilitator. Facilitation will be enabled by:

- continually throwing the discussion ball back to the group
- probing when insufficient comment is made by a member
- seeking the views of members who are not contributing
- ensuring that all can be heard and are understood
- protecting and encouraging any minority opinions
- keeping the discussion going by, when absolutely necessary, putting in a view of your own, perhaps controversial or one that the group does not seem to be going to consider
- controlling undesirable member behaviours – domination, interrupting, excessive talking, aggression, opting out, etc – in the most effective manner, but only if the group is suffering as a result of

these behaviours and does not appear to intend to take any action themselves
- summarizing at intervals when the discussion appears to be flagging or understanding is failing in a complex discussion.

Concluding the Discussion

The final part of the discussion leader's role is to conclude the discussion when it is clear that all relevant topics have been covered effectively, or when the allocated time has expired.

The leader should either produce a final summary which can often usefully be entered on the title and objectives flipchart sheet which has been exhibited during the discussion, or, preferably, have the group itself produce the summary, supported by you as necessary from the notes you will have been keeping during the discussion.

Ensure that the summary is an accurate account of what actually happened, rather than what was hoped for or intended to happen. Be careful when giving the group the task of summarizing that the result is not influenced by a vocal or dominant majority or minority at the expense of the real decisions.

DESIGN APPLICATION 38

- The input and various discussions about discussion groups and discussion-leading should be followed, as with the presentations section of the programme, by learner practice in running discussions.
- The learning group can be divided into two sub-groups which will work independently with their own trainers to save time (and boredom!).
- Time should be given for the learners to prepare a discussion to last about 10 minutes using the techniques discussed; the discussions should be followed by reviews, conducted principally by the learner discussion leader and the participants (a further discussion in itself) supported only as necessary by the trainer.
- The discussion subjects can be decided either from a list provided by the trainer or the learners can choose a subject from whatever source. The choice of subject will obviously be part of the review after the discussion – relevance, interest, discussability and so on.

---

12 Completing the Programme (2)

> CHAPTER SUMMARY ◁

This chapter:

- suggests further sessions that can be usefully included in a TDP
- describes the basic aspects of these sessions
- suggests material and design applications that can be included in these sessions
- considers:
  - listening
  - observation and feedback skills
  - questioning skills
  - role plays
  - videos and their effective use.

Listening

One of the more important skills that should be possessed by trainers is the ability to really listen to what the learners are saying. Without this they might be moving ahead on the wrong road, too fast, too slow and so on. But it is not easy to listen – for either trainers or learners.

Barriers to Listening

DESIGN APPLICATION 39

- Hold a discussion with the learning group to have them identify the barriers that a group of learners might have to listening. The learners can relate their own personal barriers to this discussion.

> • These can be posted on a flipchart by the trainer who will encourage discussion of the barriers where this seems necessary.

Any list so obtained is frightening when you consider how many may be working against you when you are hoping the other people are listening to the important things you have to say!

Aids to Listening

Barriers exist to be surmounted and there are practical things the trainer and the learner can do to improve their listening skills.

DESIGN APPLICATION 40

• Hold a discussion with the learning group to have them identify the ways in which listening might be improved. The learners may wish to relate their own personal techniques to this discussion.
• These can be posted on a flipchart by the trainer who will encourage discussion of the aids where this seems necessary.

Aids to listening include:

- ignore or, if possible, eliminate distracting factors – internal and external
- concentrate deliberately on what is being said
- ignore presentational failings – concentrate on the message
- look at the speaker
- try to avoid prejudices forming
- take notes, even if this is not necessary, but do not doodle
- if you have hearing difficulties, sit in an appropriate position
- if the subject is extremely important, take prior precautions, eg, no excessive drinking on the previous evening; not very late to bed, etc
- expect to hear something useful
- maintain an open mind
- listen for ideas you can develop yourself or may have to question
- sit in a 'listening' position – upright not slouched
- do not react to personally-emotive words
- look out for non-verbal messages
- ask questions if you don't understand.

Practical Reinforcement

If the basic format described above has been followed it will have consisted principally of comments by the trainer and discussion/identifications by the learners.

At this stage at least one practical activity is valuable in reinforcing the learning from the preceding inputs. A number of these activities are in existence, and if sufficient time is available, at least two approaches should be used.

Triads

The traditional activity for listening is usually known as 'Triads'. In this case the group is divided into small groups of three. At any time, two of the triad will discuss a subject, preferably one on which they do not agree. However, before any responses can be made, the individual who wants to respond must summarize what the speaker has just said. This summarizing is repeated on every occasion before a reply is given by either participant. The third member acts as observer and referee, ensuring that the rules are followed and leading a review after the conversation, which should last no more than five minutes. The members then change roles until each has taken the role of observer.

The triad activity will be followed by a full group discussion led by the trainer who will seek the significant points that have emerged.

Observation and Feedback Skills

Observation

It is frequently said in training circles that the observer sees and learns more than the participants. Whether this is true or not, observers during training events are valuable resources for the trainer. not only for the observers' own learning, but also as a support for the trainer during feedback and review sessions. If multiple activities are taking place, the trainer cannot be in all the places at the same time – the observers can take his or her place.

Whoever may be observing, it is essential that the observers are fully aware of their duties and responsibilities. This definition of role should have been determined by the trainers for themselves during the session preparation, but special action must be taken to ensure that learner-observers have a similar awareness.

What an observer will be looking for will depend on the type of activity. The types of activities when observation should be made will include:

- presentations
- role plays
- games and activities
- negotiations
- discussion-group leading
- problem-solving group activities.

During the periods of observation certain aspects will be observed – again these will depend on the particular activity but generally will include:

- content (the task)
- process (how it is performed)
- organization
- time control
- the pattern of the communication
- the communication methods and effectiveness
- procedures
- behaviour
- behaviour control
- process control
- emotional issues.

Observation instruments

Aids to observation usually take the form of observation sheets which are tailored to the particular event. For example, the observation sheet for a presentation would contain different items to that for a problem-solving activity. Unless there is a particular observation instrument for the event in question, time should be given to the observers before the event starts to decide what they will be looking for or to construct a relevant observation sheet. After the activity, the observers should also be given time to bring their observations together before being required to report.

The principal criterion in the construction of observation instruments is to keep them as short as possible without reducing their value in any way.

DESIGN APPLICATION 41

- Hold an activity to enable the learners to practise observation of an event. A 'fishbowl' activity can be held with half the group performing an activity and the other half observing. Decisions should be made by the observer group about what they are to observe, and an observation sheet for that particular activity provided or constructed.

- The activity should then take place and the observers report back on what they had observed, how they did it and what lessons they had learned.
- The exercise can then be repeated with the other half of the group acting as the observers.
- An alternative approach can be for the whole group to observe a video of an activity and discuss their observations.

Feedback

The feedback of performance to learners on training events is a frequent task performed by trainers, but one of, if not *the* most difficult they will be called upon to perform. Feedback follows the observation of the learners performing tasks and is the opinion of the observer(s) on the learners' behaviour and performance.

Personal feedback activity

As a practical introduction to the giving and receiving of feedback, a personal activity can be introduced at this stage.

DESIGN APPLICATION 42

- Divide the learners into pairs and ask them to write down
  a) as many things as possible they have noticed about the other person
  b) two things about the other that they like or admire.
- Ask the pairs to tell each other what they have written down about each other – verbally, not by showing the other what has been written.
- Following the exchange of views, the pairs should be asked to tell their partner how they felt
  a) when telling the other about the general features
  b) when complimenting the other
  c) when being complimented.
- In the full group, following this paired exchange, seek important, significant and common points that may have emerged.

The purpose of feedback

The validity and purpose of feedback will often be questioned by learners. Some of the responses to these questions can include:

- to see ourselves as others see us
- helps us see/hear about the effect we have on each other

- helps awareness to develop
- allows the views of others to emerge
- re-engages the participants
- gives information which can be used in progressive development, eg, in next activity, etc
- demonstrates the way in which you might upset people and suggests more appropriate behaviours.

Effective feedback
Feedback can be given either effectively (acceptably) or ineffectively (unacceptably), the latter not always being simply the negative of the former.

DESIGN APPLICATION 43

- Divide the learning group into two sub-groups – one to discuss and list the elements of effective feedback, the other the ineffective aspects. (Suggest that it might help them to think about feedback they have given or been given themselves.)
- Each group should present their results to the other and compare the flipchart listings.

The listings should include all or some of the following:

Effective actions
- be clear about what you want to say
- give feedback as soon as possible after the events
- give praise feedback first
- give positive, not negative feedback
- be specific
- concentrate on behaviours that can be changed and seek/offer alternatives
- be descriptive rather than evaluative
- own the feedback – use 'I', 'In my opinion', 'As I saw it'
- understanding of the feedback should be checked
- action should be agreed.

Ineffective actions
- being too critical
- being too soft when directness/straight speaking is obviously needed

- too soon – let the learners return to the real world after the activity
- too late
- too rushed
- too many criticisms – no more than three or four
- inappropriate feedback
- contradictory (particularly from more than one trainer)
- not actionable
- non-specific
- too theoretical
- too prescriptive
- too subjective – 'I felt'
- incomprehensible/jargon-ridden.

Structure

Particularly for those new to feedback, it is more effective to follow a structure to the feedback approach. Such a structure can be offered to the learners as an input or constructed by the learners through open discussion or sub-group activities. A model structure might include the following stages:

Before the feedback
1. Determine specific areas to observe for eventual feedback
2. Determine who is to do the activity observation and who will give the feedback
3. Arrange observers as necessary.

During the feedback
1. Observe actions and behaviours
2. Make extensive notes, preferably with examples of incidents and behaviours
3. Do not intervene or interrupt the activity, except in the most extreme circumstances.

After the event
1. Give the participants time to return to the real world
2. Give all learners time to complete a post-activity questionnaire
3. Invite the main participant to comment on their own performance
4. Invite observer(s) to comment, not necessarily following exactly the pattern of the observation sheet
5. Invite minor participant to comment (eg the interviewee in a role-play activity)
6. Trainer should perform a sweep-up feedback on any significant comments not made (aim for honesty but not over-completeness) giving any praise not given earlier and providing a summary

7. Trainer should ask participant for views
   – on feedback given
   – main points accepted

   – what they would do differently in future.

The two sides of feedback
Comment on the fact that both sides of feedback must be taken into account – the giving **and** the receiving. If the receiver is not in the mood to accept the feedback, however well it is given, most of it will be wasted. The question of attitude towards receiving feedback can be a problem for most people, but if it is to be received, a range of attitudes must be present. Let us concentrate on personal attitudes and how we can receive feedback in the most acceptable way.

DESIGN APPLICATION 44

● Seek from the group suggestions about how feedback might be received in the most effective manner and enter these on a flipchart.

The suggestions should include the following:
- listen actively and carefully
- try to avoid defensiveness
- avoid rationalizing
- be open-minded
- remember feedback represents the perceptions of the giver only
- check your understanding of what has been said
- ask questions for clarification
- seek feedback from other 'observers'
- carefully evaluate the accuracy and potential of what has been said
- consider how the feedback can help you to improve.

Rationalizing
It is only too easy to try to rationalize away feedback which you find personally unwelcome, perhaps because you see it as threatening, inaccurate, given by someone who you feel is not as aware as they should be, resulting from an unnatural situation, and so on. Mankind has an infinite capacity to find infinite ways to excuse itself in almost any situation! Typical statements by learners when trying to rationalize feedback can include:

- 'I didn't have enough time, so that's why I didn't'
- 'Of course, I wouldn't do that back at work'
- 'I didn't have enough time to prepare'
- 'Because it was a training exercise it was too artificial'
- 'I wouldn't say that in a real meeting'
- 'There wasn't time to do justice to the task'
- 'The subject matter didn't lend itself to that sort of activity'
- 'I wasn't sure what you wanted me to do'
- 'I've always done it like that and nobody has ever complained'
- 'I've always been told to do it like that'
- 'I didn't think you really wanted us to do the task, only to get the general points'
- 'It seemed to me there wasn't anything else to do'
- 'Nobody else seemed to know anything, so I didn't want to appear big-headed'
- 'There wasn't time to ask questions'
- 'X had done this before, and that put me off'
- 'After all, it was only a training exercise!'.

Questioning Skills

Linked to, and as important as discussion to help the learner produce effective training events, are the skills of effective questioning. These skills have many similarities to those used in other people contacts – appraisal, counselling, interviewing generally and so on – so the concepts will not be completely strange to the learners.

Training Questions

Questions are asked during training sessions by both the trainer and the learners.

From trainers:
- to simulate active learning
- to help learners use their own powers of learning
- to encourage experience to emerge and be shared with others
- to check understanding
- to check existing knowledge
- to have them tell you rather than the other way round
- to get participants to talk.

From learners:
- to cover gaps in their own learning
- to correct non-understanding
- to check understanding
- for further interest
- to be an active participant.

Types of Questions

Closed questions – these normally require (and obtain) a simple answer 'yes' or 'no' or straightforward statement of facts.

Presumptive questions – these are usually closed questions that assume part of the answer.

Leading questions – these tend to be negatively presumptive questions that obviously suggest that the questioner is expecting a certain answer. This may put the other person on the spot, depending on their relationship with the questioner.

Multiple questions – these are in fact a series of questions strung together. They can cause problems for the responder who may not remember all the parts of the question and consequently (or sometimes deliberately) answer one part only – usually the last part.

Rambling questions – similar to the multiple question but without the specifically identifiable parts of that type of question. The rambling question goes on and on until the listener is unsure what is being asked.

Conflict questions – these are designed to produce a reaction from the other person and may (whether intended or not) produce a negative or emotional response. If an emotional response does not emerge, it may be that emotions are present but are being suppressed.

Hypothetical questions – usually intended to test a responder's problem-solving ability by posing a hypothetical situation. This type of question *can* test ability and knowledge, but being hypothetical may receive only a hypothetical response.

Open questions – usually begin with *what, how, why,* and less openly, *who, where* and *when.* They are used to open up the discussion as the response is less likely to be monosyllabic. They can also be an invitation to give extended information.

Probing questions – these are open questions which seek further or clarified information on responses already given.

Testing understanding – a variation on the probing question that sets out to ensure that the questioner has put over a point correctly, the other person has understood what the questioner has asked or said, or the questioner has understood what the responder has said.

145

Reflection – this does not appear as a question, but its basic intention is to encourage the responder to give more information without having to be asked a question directly. If the other person has made a brief comment such as, 'I'm having some problems with the new procedure', but appears unwilling to extend this information, a reflection might be 'It seems that the problem is mainly with the new procedure'. Hopefully, the other person will then say 'Yes, that's right. What I am being asked to do is ...'.

A simple approach to using some of these questions during a training event can follow this model:

- start with simple open questions to get the participants talking
- follow up with probing questions
- extend the depth of the discussion with open questions of a more penetrating nature, followed up as necessary by probing questions
- finish with closed questions or testing understanding to confirm learning.

Dealing with Responses

Not all responses are what the questioner expects and on occasions can be difficult ones. This can be likened to the tourist trying out the language of the other country with a resident and being faced by a rapidly spoken response which is impossible or difficult to interpret.

Some of the situations that arise and that can be discussed either by the full learning group or in sub-group activities are when:

- the answer is incorrect or incomplete
- the answer is woolly but the responder had the correct answer in mind
- the question is received with silence
- the response asks for the trainer's views
- a frequent responder gives a quick, correct answer.

Whatever the response, always check before moving on that everybody is satisfied with the response(s) and summarize the position as necessary.

Activity

Following the discussion it is useful to include some form of practical activity, usually in an interviewing format during which the learners have to ask each other questions. There are many resources available that will give material for this type of inclusion.

During the session, particularly at the stage when the different types of questioning techniques are being discussed, a video might be introduced, if time permits. Several videos relating to questioning exist, but my preferred one is 'Good Question' published as a video-based training package by Fenman (originally Wyvern Business Training).

Role Plays

Role plays involve the learners in training course situations where they may have to take on a role, either an artificial one or one based on their own experience or the experience of other learners. The role play might take place in a one-to-one interaction or in a group. The principal basis is learning by doing.

The first piece of advice is *not* to use the phrase 'role play' with learning groups: often it has unfortunate connotations. It suggests a completely artificial situation and is an emotive phrase for many learners.

A useful starting point for a session on this subject is to have the learners identify, from role plays they have observed or taken part in, the problems that can emerge. These will include:

- they are time-consuming
- they can be seen as artificial
- they can become boring
- sometimes people picked to perform a role play are the wrong type
- reluctant volunteers do not enter fully into the role
- briefs for the roles have to be sufficient, but not overlong
- people see it as acting
- learners refuse to take part
- the group refuses to take part
- role players dry up during the activity
- the trainer needs skill to produce an effective review and feedback after the event
- role players may go off in an entirely different direction than that required by the brief.

DESIGN APPLICATION 45

- Divide the learning group into two groups and:
  a) ask each group to select one problem from the problems list
  b) decide how this problem would be dealt with
  c) set up a role play situation involving all the group members demonstrating the proposed method for dealing with the problem – the roles can be those of trainers controlling the role play, the role players and an observer to give feedback.

- The role play has to last no longer than 15 minutes, including any feedback which will concentrate principally on the role of the trainers.
- Allow 30 minutes for this preparation.
- Have each group perform their role play, followed by a short discussion on the significant points that emerged.

The Role of the Trainer in Role Plays

The trainer has a vital, but principally background role to play – the activity is for the learners to perform, with the trainer acting as facilitator. Elements of this role can be identified and discussed by the learners in design application 46.

DESIGN APPLICATION 46

- Divide the learning group into three sub-groups, each to consider one of the following aspects of the trainer's role in role plays:
  a) before the role play begins
  b) during the role play
  c) after the role play.
- The comments should be listed on a flipchart sheet for presentation to the trainer and the other groups.
- Ten minutes should be allowed for this part of the activity.
- Each group will present its findings and the trainer should lead a discussion.

The points emerging should include:

Before the role play
- brief the participants
- give enough background material but not too much
- decide who are to be the players (volunteers, selected learners, trainers, everyone)
- inform everybody of time allowed for preparation and for the role play
- ask role players to keep their briefs to themselves
- confirm the confidentiality of the role play and the later destruction of tapes or videos
- select and brief observers on their roles
- ask participants to behave as naturally as possible within the brief.

During the role play
- the trainer must keep quiet, watch, listen and take notes
- avoid cutting the role play short, but give time warning if previously agreed
- be prepared for some action if participant(s) dry up
- intervene as a last resort.

After the role play
- thank the participants
- ask the lead participant to comment first in feedback session
- take comments from the observers
- ask other participant(s) to comment
- seek any other views
- wherever possible, use the role names not those of the participants
- summarize, drawing out the learning points and leaving the participants with positive comments, even if only congratulating them on being brave enough to take part.

Videos and their Effective Use

Videos, both commercial and in-house, can play an important part in training, but they are too often misused. The subject of videos can be introduced with an activity designed to bring out the knowledge and experience of the learners with videos, either as trainers or learners.

DESIGN APPLICATION 47

- Divide the group into two sub-groups with the following briefs:
  Sub-group 1: What advantages do you see in using videos in training and how and when would you use them?
  Sub-group 2: What potential problems or disadvantages do you see in using videos in training and how would you avoid them?
- Allow about 15 minutes for this activity.
- Ask the sub-groups to present their findings and extend these with discussion.

The presentations should include:

Advantages –
- opportunity to model appropriate behaviour and range of behaviour

- can have high impact
- introduces variety into the presentation
- professional approach
- non-threatening
- can promote discussion
- changes the pace of the training
- gives trainer/learners breathing/thinking time.

When and how to use –
- at the start of the session to introduce
- during the session to break up the session and reinforce or introduce points
- at end of session to summarize
- as 'triggers'
- as an evening 'session'
- when session is becoming heavy.

Disadvantages –
- equipment is required
- equipment inadequate
- not always work-related/relevant
- can be seen as too general
- can be seen as too simplistic
- expensive (purchase or loan on a small number of occasions)
- some will be quickly outdated
- rooms not always suitable
- maximum number of participants depending on monitor size
- hire period – necessity for trainer to be familiar with content.

Preparation

Comments should be made that to ensure the effective use of videos, the trainer must make adequate preparations before the session in which the video is to be shown.

A summary of these preparations will include:

- equipment – familiarization with TV monitor, videorecorder and remote control if used; set or re-set counter as necessary
- view the video to familiarize yourself with its content and timing
- decide on insertion point
- design appropriate introduction
- is it to be used straight through or stopped at intervals? Identify stopping points
- is it to be used as a trigger? Commercial trigger video or self-prepared

- consider review – what is to be included and what relationships are to be made to the training and to the learners' work
- check that equipment works; volume, etc are correct; tape is wound to start or appropriate point.

Reviewing the Video Presentation

Effective action following the showing of the video, particularly if it has been shown without any interruptions, is as essential as the pre-showing preparation.

As with virtually every training activity, a considerable amount of learning takes place after the video has been shown – not everybody has picked up the learning points or some may have misinterpreted them. A discussion following the video presentation can supplement or reinforce the intended learning.

The trainer must hold a significant review which has been well planned, planned as carefully as any other part of the learning process – what subjects should be raised; what questions should be asked; how will it become evident if the video has had a learning value? The review should encourage reflection of what was seen; to lead the learners into a full consideration of the messages given, possible alternative approaches to what happened, or different responses to those given; and then to have the group relate the video message to their own situation and how they would apply the learning – in other words, the Learning Cycle in review.

An alternative approach

Some trainers find problems, however, in conducting such a discussion. An alternative is to:

- Divide the learning group into several buzz or sub-groups to discuss the video and identify and list the significant learning points. The results can then be more easily discussed following presentation by the groups
- Control the pace of the learning process by giving the learners time to return to the 'real' world after the video. Issue a question-naire through which they may marshal their thoughts about the video before entering what will be meaningful discussion.

Trigger Videos

Trigger videos which are short scenarios intended to initiate discussions should be described and demonstrated to extend the knowledge of the learners who may not have previously encountered this form of video.

You will need two commercial videos with trigger sequences, or, preferably, ones that the organization has had made (either profession-ally or in-house). Either should contain sufficient triggers so that each group has a number from which to select.

DESIGN APPLICATION 48

- Divide the learning group into two sub-groups.
- Provide each group with one video containing several triggers.
- Ask the groups to:
  - view the triggers given to the group
  - select sufficient triggers to run a discussion for seven to ten minutes
  - plan the discussion which will be with the other group and some members of the organizing group.
- Allow about 30 minutes for this part of the activity.
- Each sub-group will then run its discussion session using the triggers selected, in accordance with the planned action.
- The trainer should lead a review and feedback session concerned with:
  a) the discussions
  b) the use of triggers
  c) the subject overall.

Other Subjects

It may be necessary to include other subjects in addition to those described in this and the previous chapter. For example, the new trainer may be required, early in his or her work, to be involved with information technology and training for this subject; or the full training group might be strongly involved with one-to-one instruction. Consequently, these subjects must be included in the programme, excluding perhaps some subjects that will not be required immediately. The basic criterion must be followed, however – only include subjects that the new trainers will need in their early days as a trainer; further skills can be added when the need arises.

On the other hand, some programmes may be required for trainers who are not new, having some experience but not having received any training. My experience with many trainers of this ilk shows that, if offered, the majority welcome a programme of this nature. Some may have operated in a limited area of training but are to expand their range; others may feel they have fallen into bad habits; and yet others may feel that a programme of this type would be a welcome refresher. If these groups of trainers are to enter the programme, there may need to be significant modification, although I have found that the basic programme described, with one or two small variations, is quite acceptable to them.

13 The Last Morning

▷   CHAPTER SUMMARY   ◁

This chapter:

- suggests a format for the final morning of the two-week course
- describes the inclusion of a 'way ahead' session
- suggests the completion of end-of-course validation reviews and action planning
- discusses the problem of 'reporting-back' on the learners.

Introduction

Every training programme has to come to a close and it can often be difficult to decide what should be done at this stage. In a two-week programme such as that recommended in this book, the second workshop will probably end at about midday on the final day. There is a strong temptation to try to squeeze as much training into the limited time available, and this is where the problems often arise. You must consider whether the learners are in a mental and physical state to accept more learning. The previous day may have been taken up with the major team presentations suggested – a stretching and exhausting exercise; there may have been a 'last night' party; being the last morning, thoughts may be more inclined to returning home than further learning. I have encountered all these attitudes and only rarely have I come across complete motivation to continue learning at the pace followed in the preceding part of the programme.

The organization may insist on a full learning programme in which case the trainer must, after trying to describe the problems, continue the training, making it as interesting as possible – but knowing that little learning will in fact take place.

Information Technology in Training

Information technology and its inclusion and influence in training were mentioned at the end of Chapter 12 as a possible subject for the programme. This stage in the event can be an ideal opportunity for some learning activities in this area. The subject can be introduced with a description of what information technology is and what its place is in the organization. Future developments can be discussed and the prior experience of any learners themselves can be utilized.

But, if possible, a valuable extension of these discussions can be a hands-on period with whatever hardware can be obtained and copies of the software in use in the organization. The computers can be set up, loaded with a variety of relevant software and, with an 'expert' on hand, the learners can be given the opportunity to 'play' with the equipment. This may be the first opportunity that some learners will have had to use the technology and, if there are individuals who are going to be strongly involved in this form of training, arrangements can be suggested or made for them to receive more specific training.

The Way Ahead

The TDP workshops are the start of a continuing process of development with most of this in the learner's future. Consequently, a relevant subject to discuss at this stage is what is ahead for the learners. This can be either a role progress description – planned development, further training and so on – or it can take the form of a 'keynote' presentation by a guest speaker who might be senior in the organization to discuss with the learners how the senior management views training in the organization; changes coming that will have a relevance to training; other changes in the organization and so on. The guest speaker should be chosen with care!

End-of-programme Validation

The end of course/programme questionnaire is a validation instrument, *not* a 'happiness sheet'. The programme trainers will want information about the validity of the event, particularly if the workshops just finishing are part of a newly developed programme. The questionnaire used should be considered carefully before introduction and it should have a high validity factor itself. A recommended end of programme question-naire is included in *The Trainer Development Programme* (Leslie Rae, Kogan Page, 1994). The principal criterion for its construction must be an assessment of the *learning* achieved – has the programme achieved its aims and objectives for a learning process and have the learners actually achieved learning in the programme? This means that many of the questions asked in the all-too-common 'happiness sheet' are irrelevant and bring end-of-course validation approaches into disrepute. A second criterion is that space must always be given for the learner to add comments to any rating scale included – they should also be *encouraged* to comment rather than be faced with an invitation to comment almost 'if they feel like it'.

Another major criterion for the end-of-programme validation ques-tionnaire is that the learners must be aware that it is a valuable and useful document which will help the trainers and the organization, not to mention learners who will attend subsequent programmes. Sufficient time must be given for adequate completion following an introduction which will stress the importance of the questionnaire. Commonly the learners are handed the questionnaire as they are on the point of leaving – this clearly indicates the lack of importance that the trainers appear to afford it.

Action Planning

An end-of-programme questionnaire which concentrates on the learning achieved leads naturally to the next stage – the commitment to taking development action and the completion of action plans. These can take many forms but my prime aim for any action plan is that it should be as short and as simple as possible. The minimum requirements are:

- what the learner intends to do on return to work
- how they intend to do it
- when they intend to start and how long they will allocate to its implementation
- who else might be brought into the implementation
- what resources will be required.

A number of options for action planning are available:

- the learners can complete their individual action plans and take them away with them from the programme
- two copies can be made, one being retained by the learners, the other by the trainer who will contact the learner at an agreed date to discuss action progress.

Whichever of the alternatives is chosen, the action planning process can be helped by a sharing of views among the learners. When the plan has been drafted, each learner can pair with another and the two plans can be discussed and modified as necessary. This approach has the value that the views of another learner might suggest additional or different actions.

Individual Interviews

Many new trainers who attend trainer development programmes and who suffer the traumas of presentation practice, will have received some feedback following their presentations, but seek more feedback, given privately and possibly of a more searching nature than that given in public.

Counselling interviews of this nature can be *offered* to the learners during the last morning, a useful time being when the validation and development self-assessment questionnaires and action plans are being completed. These activities can be followed while the learners, in turn, can meet a trainer to discuss their progress, skill achievements and future needs.

The End of the Programme

The culture and attitudes of the organization will often determine how a training programme should be ended. Some organizations, and trainers, require a simple, short 'thank you for taking part and good luck' approach. Others expect a 'performance type' ending mastered by the trainers – this can take many forms, including one that I have seen used successfully with the trainer, to the accompaniment of relevant music, scrolling an acetate roll on which have been drawn incidents and characters from the course. Yet other trainers close the event with one of the many behavioural activities which can become quite emotional. Perhaps the best advice is to use an ending with which you feel comfortable *but don't be frightened to experiment.*

Reporting-back on the Learners

This is a controversial subject but one with which many trainers have to contend. Should a report on the learners be given to their managers after the end of the programme?

In some organizations the decision about this is taken out of the hands of the trainers with statements that either a report is definitely required (and in what form) or such a report is not required (and perhaps may not be welcome). In others, the trainer is given no guidance and a decision is left to them. The solution is not clear cut. If the trainer decides that no report-back should be made, but one of the learners is seen to be so incapable that something *should be said*, should it in fact become an exception?

The TDP trainer must remember that most of the learners passing through the event will be new trainers who may have experienced many aspects of training for the first time. Is it possible to make an objective comment on a person learning under such conditions over such a short period of time? I believe that (a) although the trainer can hold a belief, a fully objective assessment is very difficult to make and (b) surely it is up to the learner's manager to assess ability.

Whatever the decision or requirement, if at all possible the learners should be made aware of what is happening – failure to do this can give rise to suspicion which in turn leads to over-participation or withdrawal depending on the nature of the learner. It may be suggested that you do not tell the learners that they are to be reported on – this will obviously be a matter of conscience for the trainer, but it certainly goes against the present philosophy of openness in employment and relationships. Also, the trainer's credibility is gone forever if the learner eventually discovers that a report has been made – this could certainly affect any future training events in which the trainer and the learner have to interact.

Conclusion

By this point the training programme has been completed. Obviously its success depends not only on the relevance of the content but also on the skill and attitudes of the programme trainers and the motivation to learn on the part of the learners. A TDP can follow the one recommended in this guide, or can vary to a greater or lesser extent. I can only repeat my earlier advice – include what is *necessary*, not everything that a trainer will ever need, what the trainer's favourite subjects are, even what the organization says should be included if this is based on ignorance of training and development methods. Also remember that a training programme usually only opens doors and is not the ultimate word on any subject – real learning comes with practice of what has been learned on a programme; this can only happen at work. But at least the learner–trainer approaches these work situations with a few more skills and a little more confidence than if they had not attended an effective TDP.

Appendix: A Suggested Trainer Development Programme

The contents of this book describe material sufficient to produce a two-week, basic core skills programme. It will be necessary for the training programme designers to use their knowledge of the skill of the learners, the real time available, the organizational culture and the trainers' preferences and skills to select the relevant material to be tailored to suit the situation. One fact is certain – there will *never* be enough time available to do everything that should be done!

The suggested programme given below is based on actual trainer development programmes in which I have been involved as either the designer, the trainer or both. These programmes were all different, principally because of the skill and experience mix on the courses – from a completely new trainer who had been appointed only that day to trainers having five years and more experience, but who had worked in restricted environments and had not received previous training – for example, I came across one trainer of five years' standing who, because of the type of training she had been performing, had not used an OHP, but would, because of a change, soon have this pleasure!

The complete programme suggested is one which starts with an open learning induction pack which the learners and their managers receive prior to the workshop programmes. The workshop programme is attended at the earliest opportunity following the appointment and completion of the induction pack. This consists of two basic core skills courses, separated by an interval of about two months, the basic skills being modelled on the requirements of TDNVQ Level 3. During the following months, one- and two-day modules are offered as required, covering specific and more advanced training skills, until by the end of an 18-month period the new trainer will have covered most of the NVQ competences with the exception of some of the more global requirements.

The following programme relates to the two-week course and is intended to run from just before lunch on the Monday to about noon on the following Friday on both weeks. Ideally, the course is residential and the learners should be prepared to work on most days from 9 am to about 7 pm. I have found that although this is tiring, committed, new trainers do not feel that excessive demands are being made on them in the circumstances.

With a group of 10 to 12 learners, two trainers is the recommended cadre.

Workshop 1

Day 1

1200 – 1300	Introduction to programme and learner introductions.
Lunch	
1400 – 1445	Introduction continued. Learner expectations, description of learning logs activity and first completion of the self-assessment three-test.*
1445 – 1700 (including break)	The role of the trainer – selected material.
1700 – 1730	Trainer qualifications (if relevant).
1730 – 1900	Adult learning – barriers, learning recall, etc. (The learning styles questionnaire can be issued for evening completion, without any explanation other than intructions for completion; learners should be told that the results will be discussed on the next day). The learners will be asked to complete their Learning Log for this first day during the evening.

Day 2

0900 – 0930	Brief presentation of learning log entries in two parallel sub-groups.

*Used principally as a self-assessment test, the three-test extends the traditional pre-test/post test procedure. A self-assessment questionnaire is completed at the start of the training and at the end, as with pre-test and post-test, but the learner is also asked to repeat the first questionnaire, a procedure which reflects a more realistic self-awareness as well as enhanced knowledge. (For a fuller description of the three-test, see *The Trainer Development Programme*, Kogan Page, 1994 or *How to Measure Training Effectiveness*, Second Edition, Gower, 1991; both by Leslie Rae.)

0930 – 1030	Adult learning – analysis of learning styles and related activity.
1045 – 1215	Communication – methods, problems and barriers and activity.
1215 – 1315	Non-verbal communication – selected according to prior experience and learning of learners.
Lunch	
1415 – 1445	Period for final preparation for mini-presentations.
1445 – 1630	Mini-presentations (group divided into two parallel-operating sub-groups).
1630 – 1800	Activities in training.
	The learners will be asked to complete their learning log for this second day during the evening.

Day 3

0900 – 0930	Brief presentation of learning log entries in two parallel sub-groups.
0930 – 1100	Questioning skills (selected activities).
1115 – 1300	Preparing a script (may include part-preparation of learners' briefs for their 20-minute presentation if time is available).
	(Inclusion of some material will depend on (a) the time available and (b) the needs of the learners.)
Lunch	
1400 – 1600	Visual aids including hands-on experience or sub-group presentations.
1600 –	Preparation time for the 20-minute talks. This should be allowed to continue to any time in the evening that the individuals require, with workshop trainer support. The learners should also be expected to complete their learning log during the evening.

Day 4

0900 – 1015	Presentation skills.
1015 – 1045	Break.
1045 –	20-minute presentations in two parallel sub-groups. Two presentations before lunch, three or four after lunch depending on size of learning group.
	If time is available, a discussion can be held to bring out the significant points that emerged during the presentations.

Day 5

0900 – 1015	Listening skills.
1015	Break.
1030 –	Conclusion – completion of final learning log, sheets two and three of the three-test, and of the personal action plan. If mechanism exists to follow-up learners, an end-of-workshop validation questionnaire can be issued for completion and return soon after the workshop. If there is no such mechanism, completion should be at this stage of the workshop.

WORKSHOP 2

Day 1

1200 – 1430 (including lunch)	Re-introduction of the programme and discussion of the experiences during the period between the two workshops.
1445 – 1700 (including break)	Training objectives.
1700 –	Reminder about learning log and first day completion.

Day 2

0900 – 0940	Presentation of learning log entries and discussion in two parallel sub-groups.
0940 – 1200	Observation and feedback skills.
Lunch	
1300 – 1500	Role plays.
1515 – 1600	CCTV and its place in training.
1600 – 1730	Videos and their use in training.
1730 –	Learning log completion.

Day 3

0900 – 1245	Discussion-leading as a training technique.
1245 –	Team presentation preparation (to end of day as determined by the learners; including lunch and afternoon breaks).

Day 4

0900 –   Team presentations.

Day 5

0900 – 1030   Technology and other techniques in training.
1030 – 1200   Validation, evaluation and action planning, to closure.

Recommended Further Reading

Below you will find a list of books and other publications which you may find useful in extending the guidance given in this book. The list has been limited to those publications which are well-known, relatively recently published and easy to obtain. For ease of subject identification, the publication title has been given first (in alphabetical order), followed by the author's name, then the publisher and year of publication.

Annual Handbooks for Group Facilitators, Pfeiffer and Jones, University Associates/Pfeiffer, annually from 1972

Assessing Trainer Effectiveness, Leslie Rae, Gower, 1991

Coaching, Mentoring and Assessing, Eric Parsloe, Kogan Page, 1992

A Compendium of Icebreakers, Energizers and Introductions, edited by Andy Kirby, Gower, 1993

Developing Effective Training Skills, Tony Pont, McGraw-Hill, 1991

Effective Feedback Skills, Tim Russell, Kogan Page, 1994

Evaluating Training Effectiveness, Peter Bramley, McGraw-Hill, 1991

Guide to In-Company Training Methods, Leslie Rae, Gower, 1992

Handbooks of Structured Experiences for Human relations Training, Pfeiffer and Jones, University Associates/Pfeiffer, various

How to Design and Introduce Induction Training Programmes, Michael Meighan, Kogan Page, 1991

How to Develop and Present Staff Training Courses, Peter R Sheal, Kogan Page, 1989.

How to Measure Training Effectiveness, Leslie Rae, Gower, 1991

How to Talk so People Listen, Sonya Hamlin, Thorsons, 1989

How to Write and Prepare Training Materials, Nancy Stimson, Kogan Page, 1991

Icebreakers, Ken Jones, Kogan Page, 1991

Improving Training Effectiveness, edited Roger Bennett, Gower, 1988

Learning Style Inventory (*Experiential Learning: Experience as a Source of Learning and Development*), David A Kolb, Prentice-Hall, 1984

The Manual of Learning Styles, Peter Honey and Alan Mumford, Peter Honey, 1992

National Standards for Training and Development, Training and Development Lead Body, 1991 and 1994

NVQs Standards and Competence, Shirley Fletcher, Kogan Page, 1991

One-to-One Training and Coaching Skills, Roger Buckley and Jim Caple, Kogan Page, 1991

A Practical Approach to Group Training, David Leigh, Kogan Page, 1991

Role Plays, David Turner, Kogan Page, 1992

Running an Effective Training Session, Patrick Forsyth, Gower, 1992

Selecting and Using Training Aids, David Flegg and Josephine McHale, Kogan Page, 1991

The Skills of Human Relations Training, Leslie Rae, Gower, 1985

Teaching Hard, Teaching Soft, Colin Corder, Gower, 1990

Techniques of Training, Leslie Rae, Gower, 1993

The Trainer's Desk Reference, Second Edition, Geoffrey Moss, Kogan Page, 1993.

The Trainer Development Programme, Leslie Rae, Kogan Page, 1994

The Trainer Grid, John Townsend, Journal of European Industrial Training, Vol 9, No 3, 1985

The Trainer's Pocketbook of Ready-to-use Exercises, John Townsend, Management Pocketbooks, 1993

The Training Quadrant, Bennett, Jones and Pettigrew, MSC/ITD Guide to Trainer Effectiveness, 1984

Training Methods that Work, Lois B Hart, Kogan Page, 1991

Training Needs Analysis in the Workplace, Robyn Peterson, Kogan Page, 1992.

Using Video in Training and Education, Ashly Pinnington, McGraw-Hill, 1992

Other bibliographies and lists of recommended reading are included in the publications listed above.

'Activities' are covered in a wide range of activity collections published by BACIE, Connaught, Gower, Fenman, Kogan Page, Longman, McGraw-Hill, Melrose, Pfeiffer, *et al.* For an article commenting on these and their selection and use, see 'Activities for Trainers – bane or boon', Leslie Rae, *Training Officer*, Vol 29, No 10, December 1993.

Index